100
women
who made
history

Remarkable women who shaped our world

This book is dedicated to Lin Esposito

DK London

Senior project editor
Steven Carton

Senior art editors
Jacqui Swan, Laura Gardner

Jackets coordinator Claire Gell

Jacket design development manager
Sophia MTT

Producer, pre-production
Jacqueline Street

Producers
Mary Slater, Anna Vallarino

Managing editor Lisa Gillespie

Managing art editor Owen Peyton Jones

Publisher Andrew Macintyre

Associate publishing director
Liz Wheeler

Art director Karen Self

Design director Phil Ormerod

Publishing director Jonathan Metcalf

DK Delhi

Senior editor Sreshtha Bhattacharya

Project editor Priyaneet Singh

Project art editor Shreya Anand

Assistant editor Charvi Arora

Assistant art editors Nidhi Rastogi,
Garima Sharma, Saloni Dhawan

Jacket designers
Suhita Dharamjit, Surabhi Wadhwa

Jacket editorial coordinator
Priyanka Sharma

Senior DTP designers
Harish Aggarwal, Jagtar Singh

DTP designers
Pawan Kumar, Mohammad Rizwan

Senior picture researcher Sumedha Chopra

Managing jackets editor Saloni Singh

Picture researcher manager Taiyaba Khatoon

Pre-production manager Balwant Singh

Production manager Pankaj Sharma

Managing editor Kingshuk Ghoshal

Managing art editor Govind Mittal

First published in Great Britain in 2017 by
Dorling Kindersley Limited
80 Strand, London WC2R 0RL

Copyright © 2017 Dorling Kindersley Limited
A Penguin Random House Company
10 9 8 7
011 – 294589 – February/2017

A CIP catalogue record for this book
is available from the British Library.

ISBN: 978–0–2412–5724–1

Printed and bound in Malaysia

A WORLD OF IDEAS:
SEE ALL THERE IS TO KNOW

www.dk.com

100
women
who made
history

Remarkable women who shaped our world

Written by Stella Caldwell,
Clare Hibbert, Andrea Mills,
and Rona Skene

Consultant Philip Parker

Contents

Clued-up creatives

There's no business like show business with these leading ladies topping the bill. From the stars of stage and screen to the brains behind-the-scenes, a glittering line-up of authors, actors, and artists lights up the world of entertainment and the arts. Whether they give us painted portraits, powerhouse performances, or penned poems, their extraordinary talent is an inspiration to us all.

Very little is known about Sappho's life. Born on the **Greek island of LESBOS**, sometime between 630 and 612 BCE, she *may have married and had a daughter*. One legend tells of how Sappho threw herself off a cliff when a sailor broke her heart.

By the way...
My likeness appeared on ancient coins, and my poetry was so admired that Plato called me the "tenth muse".

The lyre is similar to a small harp, and features between four and ten strings.

How she changed...
Many poets have tried to imitate Sappho's style through the ages. Her metre, or rhythm, is named "Sapphic metre", after her.

the world

Sappho

The GREATEST FEMALE POET of the ancient world

Love poetry

As a lyrical poet, Sappho intended her verses to be sung to the music of a **LYRE**. Her poetry is often about love, and she was **one of the first poets to write about her own feelings and thoughts**. Although Sappho wrote nine volumes of poetry, *today only 650 lines of her work survive*.

Life of devotion

Raised **A PRINCESS** in 16th-century India, Mira Bai devoted her life to the Hindu **god Krishna**. When her husband died, she refused to kill herself – as was customary – and instead *escaped to live the life of a wandering saint and poet*.

Mira Bai

The SAINTLY POET-PRINCESS who was not afraid to stand up for her beliefs

Krishna is revered as a warrior and teacher by Hindus.

By the way...
Today, I am considered one of the greatest female saints in India, and my poems are sung throughout the country.

Mira Bai played a stringed instrument called the *dotara*.

How she changed...

In going against the customs of her time, Mira Bai inspired many women to lead creative and spiritual lives.

the world

Saintly poet

Mixing with the poor, Mira Bai **displayed her love for Krishna** by singing and dancing in the streets. Many were inspired by her **SELFLESS DEVOTION**. Today, about 1,300 poems in *passionate praise of Krishna* – each called a *bhajan* – are attributed to her.

Emily Dickinson

The POET who wasn't afraid to rewrite the rules

Unrecognized during her lifetime, American poet Emily Dickinson produced nearly 1,800 strikingly original poems and colourful letters.

Family life

Born in 1830 into a well-known family from Massachusetts, USA, Emily Dickinson enjoyed a **LIVELY CHILDHOOD**. *Sensitive and intelligent*, she was **adored by her two siblings**, but her relationship with her mother was frosty, and her father could be controlling.

Dickinson with her brother Austin and sister Lavinia

Did you know?
Dickinson may have suffered from either epilepsy or agoraphobia (a fear of being in public places), making her reluctant to leave home.

The solitary poet

Dickinson first wrote poetry in her teens, but she began taking it seriously around 1850, experimenting and trying out **NEW IDEAS**. As time passed, she withdrew more and more from society, but her **poetic output increased**. Despite her isolation, she *corresponded with many friends* and literary associates.

Who came before...

*The 17th-century "metaphysical" poets – including the famous **JOHN DONNE** – strongly influenced Dickinson with their direct style, wit, and striking metaphors.*

*Dickinson admired English novelist and poet **EMILY BRONTË**. One of Brontë's poems was read aloud at Dickinson's funeral.*

The "Still–volcano–life"

Dickinson's work **challenged the existing definitions of poetry**. Her poems often lacked titles, contained abrupt line breaks, made use of **STARTLING IMAGERY** – like the "still volcano" that expressed an explosive inner life – and had unexpected punctuation. She explored *themes of death and immortality*, as well as religion, time, nature, and love.

By the way...
My father tried to stop me from reading books that might "joggle" my mind!

Manuscript of Dickinson's poem *Two-were Immortal twice–*

Dickinson's love of the natural world was reflected in her poetry.

Publication

Only a few of Dickinson's poems were published during her lifetime, *anonymously*. After her death, her sister discovered **hundreds of poems**. A first volume of Dickinson's work was printed four years later. The popularity of her work, stoked by her unique way of looking at the world, has grown. Today, Dickinson is one of the **MOST WIDELY READ** American poets.

How she changed the world

Dickinson's incredibly unique life and work flew in the face of 19th-century expectations of women. She played with poetic form and used unexpected imagery, paving the way for the "modern" poets of the 20th century.

Who came after...

Dickinson's unusual poetic forms and unexpected rhythms were later echoed in the poetry of 20th-century writers such as **T. S. Eliot** *and Ezra Pound.*

Dickinson's drive to create her own poetic voice also inspired other female poets, such as **Sylvia Plath** *and Adrienne Rich.*

Screen stars

LEADING LIGHTS of the movies

Since the early days of cinema, women have had an increasingly important creative input, with these stars topping the bill.

Marlene Dietrich

German-American singer and actor Marlene Dietrich featured in the successful 1930 film *Der Blaue Engel (The Blue Angel)*. It propelled her to stardom, and she was soon whisked off to the centre of the American film industry, **HOLLYWOOD**. She went on to become one of the **highest-paid actors** of the time, and later toured the world singing and acting in theatres.

Monroe shot to fame after she was spotted working in a weapons factory in 1944.

During World War II, Dietrich helped refugees fleeing Germany and France to settle in the USA.

Marilyn Monroe

Born Norma Jeane Mortenson in 1926, **American actor Marilyn Monroe** grew up in foster homes. She took on her famous name at the start of her *glittering film career* in the 1950s, which included a win at the **GOLDEN GLOBE AWARDS**. Monroe died tragically aged 36, but she remains the ultimate glamour icon.

Kathryn Bigelow

This American writer and director is best known for her **GRIPPING FILM AND TELEVISION DRAMAS** featuring striking visuals and *slow-motion action sequences*. In 2008, Kathryn Bigelow made history by becoming the **first woman to win the Best Director award at the Oscars**, for her war-themed blockbuster, *The Hurt Locker*.

Bigelow filmed *The Hurt Locker* in Jordan.

Madhuri Dixit

Indian film star Madhuri Dixit was the queen of the Indian film industry, known as **BOLLYWOOD**, in the 1980s and 1990s, taking the lead in many screen love stories. Nominated a record-breaking 14 times for **Filmfare Awards** (a popular awards show in India), *she was the winner four times*.

Dixit is reknowned for her spectacular dance performances.

Jennifer Lawrence

The *21st century's leading lady in Hollywood*, American actor Jennifer Lawrence is famous for her **RIVETING PERFORMANCE** in the *Hunger Games* series of films. The **youngest actor to receive four Oscar nominations**, she took the prize for her role in the romantic comedy *Silver Linings Playbook* in 2013.

Josephine Baker

All-singing, ALL-DANCING freedom-fighter

Known as the "Black Pearl", Josephine Baker painted the town red, lit up the silver screen, and gathered a Rainbow Tribe.

A scene from *Shuffle Along*

A star is born

Born in 1906 in St Louis, USA, Baker left home as a teenager and joined a **VAUDEVILLE** (variety entertainment) troupe. She honed her **dancing and comedic skills** before winning a part in the Broadway musical **Shuffle Along** in 1921.

By the way...
My pet cheetah Chiquita wore a diamond-encrusted collar and caused a stir whenever we went for a walk!

French fancy

Spotted by a talent scout in 1925, **BAKER MOVED TO PARIS**, France. Her exotic style and wild dance routines made her **Europe's highest-paid performer** by 1927. Baker became a singer and actor in the 1930s, *breaking new ground for African-American women*.

What came before...

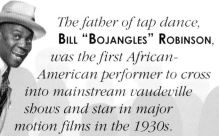

In 1891, the Creole Show in New York, USA, introduced the **CAKEWALK**, the first dance performed on stage by African-American people. This was followed by the Charleston, Jitterbug, Lindy Hop, and Twist.

The father of tap dance, **BILL "BOJANGLES" ROBINSON**, was the first African-American performer to cross into mainstream vaudeville shows and star in major motion films in the 1930s.

War and peace

During **WORLD WAR II**, the glamour girl was a spy for the French Resistance against the Nazi German forces, delivering messages. She also helped the *Red Cross* and entertained troops overseas. After the war, she adopted 12 children from around the world to prove that people of all races could **live in harmony**. She called them her "Rainbow Tribe".

Baker with some of her 12 children

Baker addressing the crowds at the Lincoln Memorial, Washington, USA

Making a stand

Baker experienced **racism and hostility** in her American homeland, so she campaigned hard for the 1960s **CIVIL RIGHTS MOVEMENT** at demonstrations and marches. Following the assassination of Martin Luther King, Jr., the movement's leader, she was *asked to take control*. She declined, believing she would be too busy to see her children.

Did you know?
When she died in 1975, Baker was the first American woman to receive full French military honours at her funeral.

How she changed the world

Josephine Baker is proof that anything is possible, turning humble beginnings into international superstardom. She lived life to the fullest, cramming in careers as a singer, dancer, actor, spy, activist, and campaigner, at a time when opportunities for African-Americans were few and far between.

Who came after...

Josephine Baker remains a style icon in the 21st century, with African-American star **BEYONCÉ** describing Baker's dance moves as inspirational and paying homage with her costumes and routines.

In 2015, **MISTY COPELAND** made history at the American Ballet Theatre Company when she became the first African-American principal dancer of the company.

Edith Piaf

The LITTLE SPARROW of Paris who became a global singing sensation

Born to perform

The **daughter of a circus acrobat** and a street singer, Edith Piaf started performing for a living in her teens. Her *speciality was the* chanson – a type of nostalgic song from the cafés of Paris. After becoming popular in France, her fame spread until she was a **GLOBAL CELEBRITY**.

Piaf visited many injured French servicemen during World War II.

How she changed...

Piaf's unique voice and dramatic style made her one of the highest-paid, most admired, and most influential performers ever.

the world

War hero

During **WORLD WAR II**, Piaf used her stardom to help German-occupied France. During a **concert in a prisoner-of-war camp**, she smuggled in false identity papers, *helping more than 300 French prisoners to escape*.

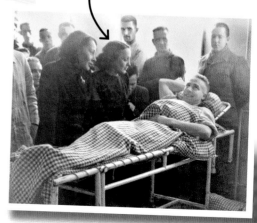

Rising star

Greek-American Maria Callas **took singing lessons from the age of five**. Her **BIG BREAK** came in 1949, when she took a leading role in an opera at Teatro la Fenice, Venice, Italy. She *learned the whole part in just six days* – and her performance was a sensation!

Present-day Teatro la Fenice

Maria Callas
The SUPERSTAR who put as much passion into her life as her art

Musical megastar

Callas was adored for her *acting performances* as well as her singing. Her charisma made opera appeal to people who had never been interested in it before. Callas's off-stage life was **FULL OF DRAMA**, too. Her glamorous looks, celebrity lifestyle, and public fights with fellow musicians meant that she was often **in the headlines**.

One of Callas's most famous roles was as tragic hero Tosca.

How she changed...

Callas's dazzling talents and style attracted millions of new fans to opera.

the world

Frida Kahlo

SELFIE-starter

Mexico's greatest female artist broke with convention by putting herself in the picture, revealing her personal struggles in self-portraits for all the world to see.

By the way...
Known as surrealism, my style of painting involved bizarre themes and imaginative subjects.

Kahlo at the age of five

Unlucky start

Bad luck plagued Frida Kahlo's early life. She **contracted polio at the age of six** and was badly injured in a bus accident as a teenager. Faced with **CONSTANT PAIN** and ongoing operations, she turned to *painting for expression and entertainment*.

Diego Rivera

Artist and activist

Kahlo was **one of the only female students** at Mexico's National Preparatory School, where she painted **DRAMATIC SELF-PORTRAITS**. With the Mexican Revolution underway, Kahlo joined the Mexican Communist Party. In 1929, she married *Mexican muralist Diego Rivera*, who shared her political views.

What came before...

The world's first portraits date back to **ANCIENT EGYPTIAN** *tomb art, sculptures, and paintings.*

With the use of mirrors in the Renaissance period, artists such as **LEONARDO DA VINCI** *began painting themselves in formal portraits.*

Inspirational icon

In 1939, Kahlo **moved to Paris**, France, where she exhibited her paintings and befriended Spanish painter Pablo Picasso and French artist Marcel Duchamp. Returning home in 1943, Kahlo began teaching at a new art school in Mexico City named **LA ESMERALDA**, where her work gained fans and followers, leading to a **solo exhibition** there in 1953.

Fight to the death

Poor health blighted Kahlo's later life, but that didn't keep her from appearing at her exhibition's opening night. **From a bed in the gallery**, Kahlo celebrated her success and spoke to the audience. She made a **LAST PUBLIC APPEARANCE** at a political rally before her death at the age of 47 at Casa Azul (Blue House), her home in Mexico City.

Kahlo's pets, including monkeys, dogs, and birds, featured regularly in her work.

Casa Azul is now a museum dedicated to Kahlo.

How she changed the world

At a time when female artists were largely ignored by critics, Kahlo broke the mould with her surrealist style. If a picture paints a thousand words, Kahlo's raw and rebellious works voiced the strengths and struggles of millions of women.

Who came after...

Spanish painter **SALVADOR DALI** was a surrealist artist with a quirky personality and a preference for self-portraiture.

Many modern female artists, including American photographer **CINDY SHERMAN**, have been influenced by Kahlo's self-portraits.

Women writers

For centuries, female writers struggled to get their work published, let alone praised. However, as these authors show, they have given us some of the greatest literature ever written.

Breaking down barriers with WORDS

Murasaki Shikibu

Shikibu's novel, *The Tale of Genji*, was finished by 1021 and is considered to be the **single greatest work of Japanese literature**. It is also one of the **WORLD'S FIRST** novels. The 54-chapter book tells the tale of Genji, the son of an ancient Japanese emperor, and is almost certainly based on Shikibu's experience of *life at court*.

"Murasaki Shikibu" is a nickname – the writer's real name is unknown.

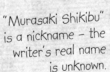

Shin Saimdang

There was nothing ordinary about this gifted artist who **OVERCAME THE RIGID BARRIERS** of 16th-century *Korean society* to excel not only at poetry, but at calligraphy, painting, and embroidery, too. As the mother of seven children, including the famous scholar Yulgok, Shin Saimdang is often celebrated as a "**wise mother**".

Mary Wollstonecraft

This British **"founder of feminism"** was way ahead of her time when she set down her revolutionary ideas about the **PLACE OF WOMEN IN SOCIETY**. In her most famous book, *A Vindication of the Rights of Women*, published in 1792, she passionately argued for girls to receive the same education as boys.

Austen received little recognition for her work in her lifetime.

Jane Austen

Set among the **English middle and upper classes**, Jane Austen's six novels – including *Sense and Sensibility*, *Pride and Prejudice*, and *Emma* – shine out for their **SHARP WIT AND WONDERFUL INSIGHT** into the *lives of 19th-century women*. Austen's books are considered literary classics today.

Maya Angelou

Best known for her painful memoir about her *extremely poor upbringing* in 1930s Arkansas, USA – *I Know Why the Caged Bird Sings* – **African-American author** Maya Angelou was also a celebrated poet and **CIVIL RIGHTS ACTIVIST**. Praised by critics far and wide, her books include many poetry and essay collections, and her seven-part autobiography.

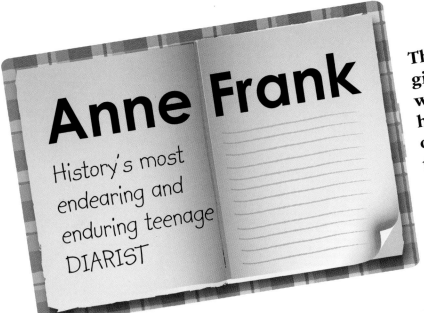

Anne Frank

History's most endearing and enduring teenage DIARIST

The young Jewish girl whose wartime writings won the hearts of millions of readers around the world.

Start of the story

Annelies Marie Frank was born in Frankfurt, Germany, in 1929. Her father, Otto Frank, fearing persecution for their **JEWISH FAITH** at the hands of the anti-Jewish Nazi party, **moved his family to the Netherlands** in 1933. Anne was educated in Amsterdam. She was a *voracious reader who excelled at writing*.

Did you know?
Originally written in Dutch, Anne's diary has been translated into more than 60 languages and sold more than 30 million copies.

Special gift

By 1940, World War II was underway. The Netherlands was **occupied by the Nazis** and the Frank family was under threat. The family tried to emigrate once again, this time to the **USA**, but this was blocked in 1941. Anne turned 13 in 1942, and *received a journal as a gift* from her parents.

Who came before...

THE CONFESSIONS OF ST AUGUSTINE OF HIPPO *are autobiographical books in Latin, in which St Augustine explored his feelings on religion and philosophy.*

Famous English diarist **SAMUEL PEPYS** *kept a diary for almost a decade, giving a valuable account of London, England, during the 17th century.*

By the way...
I named my diary "Kitty" because I thought of it as a friend in whom I could confide.

Located above Otto's Amsterdam office, the family hideaway is now the most visited place in the Netherlands.

Secret hideaway

Shortly after Anne's birthday, the family fled to a *secret living area* behind and above Otto's office. **Friends brought food supplies** and news updates. Anne relieved her boredom by recording her feelings about her family, about what was happening, and her hopes for the future. On 4 August 1944, the **NAZIS FOUND THE HIDEAWAY** and Anne's diary ended.

THE DIARY OF A YOUNG GIRL

ANNE FRANK

EDITED BY OTTO H. FRANK AND MIRIAM PRESSLER

PENGUIN READERS

Final chapter

The Frank family was taken to *Auschwitz concentration camp*. Anne was moved to Bergen-Belsen camp where **she died of typhus** in 1945. Otto survived the war and ensured Anne's diary was published in 1947. It became an international **BEST-SELLER**.

How she changed the world

Though Anne was tragically killed by the Nazis, her words, preserved in her diary, have lived on to remind us of the value and dignity of human life.

Who came after...

From 1991 to 1993, **ZLATA FILIPOVIĆ** kept a record of her experiences growing up in war-torn Sarajevo in Bosnia and Herzegovina. Her experiences were published in the book Zlata's Diary.

Today, people use **THE INTERNET** to record their thoughts on weblogs, or through social media sites.

Joni Mitchell

A SONGWRITER
whose music will play on forever

A legend in the making

Born in a remote Canadian town in 1943, Joni Mitchell always **loved art and music**. She learned to play guitar, and wrote songs with **meaningful lyrics and beautiful melodies**. She released her debut album in 1968. Mitchell's huge hits, including "Both Sides Now" and "Big Yellow Taxi", turned her into a **FOLK MUSIC LEGEND**.

Albums and awards

Mitchell won her first Grammy Award in 1969 for **BEST FOLK PERFORMANCE**. Throughout the 1970s, *she experimented with jazz, pop, and other musical genres*. Her **passion for painting** showed in the many album covers that displayed her artwork. She went on to release 19 albums and bag another eight Grammys.

How she changed...

The originality of Mitchell's music and lyrics influenced many songwriters and captivated fans around the world.

the world

J. K. Rowling

The WRITING WIZARD whose spellbinding words cast their magic over readers worldwide

Bookworm's journey

Born in 1965, Joanne Rowling grew up in Gloucestershire, UK, **surrounded by books**. At the age of six, she *wrote her first story*, about a rabbit with measles. In 1990, she dreamed up the idea for her **BOY-WIZARD, HARRY POTTER**, while delayed on a train. *Harry Potter and the Philosopher's Stone* was published seven years later.

How she changed...

A multi-award-winning author, Rowling has sold more than 450 million books in over 70 languages.

the world

Rags to riches

Children and adults alike loved the **FANTASY STORIES** set at "Hogwarts School of Witchcraft and Wizardry". More books followed in the series, all of which sold amazingly well, and Rowling became a household name. A **film deal** for the series followed, and the eight films *smashed box office records*.

25

Super

scientists

Science has welcomed many ground-breaking developments and discoveries from women. Light years ahead of their time, these pioneers of progress have conquered new ground in their chosen areas of chemistry, physics, biology, mathematics, zoology, and palaeontology. By bringing their knowledge and inventions to the forefront, they have transformed our lives for the better.

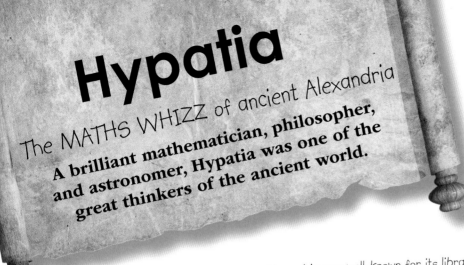

Hypatia

The MATHS WHIZZ of ancient Alexandria

A brilliant mathematician, philosopher, and astronomer, Hypatia was one of the great thinkers of the ancient world.

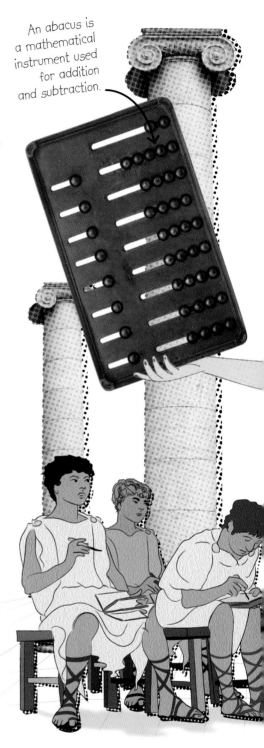

An abacus is a mathematical instrument used for addition and subtraction.

Alexandria was well-known for its library, which contained works by the greatest minds of the ancient world.

Solid foundations

Born in about 355 CE in Alexandria, an Egyptian city *famous for being a centre of learning*, Hypatia was the child of Theon, a philosopher and mathematician. Although it was unusual for the time, Theon **educated his daughter** and she **EXCELLED IN HER STUDIES**.

Charismatic teacher

Hypatia became the **leading mathematician of her era**, achieving recognition in algebra, geometry, and astronomy. She also **BUILT A REPUTATION AS AN OUTSTANDING TEACHER**, particularly of philosophy. Hypatia taught a kind of philosophy called "Neoplatonism", which, at the time, was seen as a form of paganism. Her lectures drew huge crowds, and she *played an active role in Alexandrian life*.

Who came before...

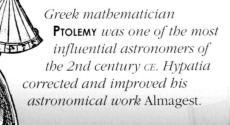

Greek mathematician **Ptolemy** *was one of the most influential astronomers of the 2nd century CE. Hypatia corrected and improved his astronomical work* Almagest.

Plotinus *was an important Neoplatonist philosopher of the ancient world. He believed that there was a supreme, supernatural entity that he called "The One".*

Grisly death

Cyril, the Christian archbishop of Alexandria, was involved in an *intense feud with the city's pagan governor*, Orestes. As the governor's friend, Hypatia became a **FOCAL POINT OF RELIGIOUS TENSION**. Things came to a head in 415 CE, when she was dragged from her carriage and **brutally murdered by a Christian mob**.

By the way...
I was so well-known that eminent thinkers travelled from many different countries to hear me lecture.

Did you know?
Alexandria was a great centre of learning for almost 800 years, but was in decline by 400 CE due to religious turmoil.

How she changed the world

Hypatia's extraordinary brilliance lay not only in her inquiring mind, but in her ability to teach complicated concepts. At a time when almost all women led lives centred around the home, she was a leading mathematician and teacher.

Who came after...

In 1786, German astronomer **CAROLINE HERSCHEL** *was the first woman to discover a comet, and the first to be paid for her scientific work.*

In 2014, Iranian-American mathematician **MARYAM MIRZAKHANI** *was the first woman and first Iranian to receive the Fields Medal (a prestigious award in mathematics).*

Émilie du Châtelet

The mathematician, physicist, and writer who played a key role in Europe's AGE OF ENLIGHTENMENT

Du Châtelet's father, Louis Nicolas le Tonnelier de Breteuil

Talented teen

Émilie du Châtelet was born into a wealthy French aristocratic family in 1706. Her father allowed her to attend his **discussion groups**, to which he invited well-known writers and thinkers. The debates **FIRED HER CURIOSITY**. She also had fencing and riding lessons, and became fluent in *Latin, Greek, German, and English*.

Advances in science

Du Châtelet's partner was the **French philosopher Voltaire**. They wrote a best-selling book together, and even set up a science laboratory at home. Her major achievement was her *French translation of Isaac Newton's great work*, *the Principia Mathematica*. In it she also **EXPLAINED AND TESTED** Newton's exciting new theories on astronomy, gravity, and the nature of light and colours.

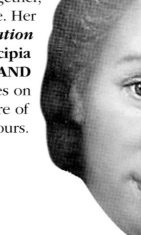

Voltaire said of his partner, "No woman was ever more learned."

How she changed... the world

By translating and building on Newton's work, du Châtelet made a massive contribution to the scientific community of her time.

By the way...
My study of how fire behaves was the first paper by a woman ever published by the Académie des Sciences in Paris.

Ada Lovelace

The trailblazer who wrote the first COMPUTER code

Charles Babbage's Analytical Engine was never built in his lifetime, but experts agree that it would have worked.

Father of computing, Charles Babbage

Babbage's Engine was designed to use punched cards to input data.

By the way...
The programming language "ADA", first created for the US Department of Defense, was named after me.

The first computer geek

As a child, Ada Lovelace developed *a passion for mathematics*. When she was 17, she met **British mathematician Charles Babbage**, who had designed the Analytical Engine – an early computer to do calculations. She devised a set of instructions, or an **ALGORITHM**, on how to make the Engine perform different tasks – making her the world's first computer programmer.

Taking a gamble

A keen **GAMBLER**, Lovelace developed a mathematical model *to beat the odds on horse races*. The scheme went **very wrong**, and she lost so much money that she secretly had to sell some family jewellery.

How she changed...
Lovelace not only wrote the first computer program, she also got people thinking about the kinds of things computers could do.

the world

31

Mary Anning

England's most formidable FOSSIL FINDER

British amateur geologist Mary Anning trawled the sands of her local beach to make discoveries that would change our understanding of evolutionary history.

Ichthyosaurus had the largest eye sockets found anywhere among vertebrate animals.

Buried treasures

Born in 1799, Mary Anning grew up in the **British seaside resort of Lyme Regis**, Dorset, England, where she **sold shells to tourists**. One memorable day, she and her brother Joseph found a **MARINE REPTILE SKELETON** on the beach, which was later identified as an ichthyosaur, or "fish-lizard".

Fossils of ammonites – ancient sea creatures with coiled shells – are common on the Jurassic Coast of England.

Did you know?
Mary was a born survivor, remaining unscathed after being hit by lightning as a baby.

Coprolites are animal droppings that have become fossilized.

Who came after...

In 1841, English anatomist RICHARD OWEN coined the term "dinosaur", which means "terrible lizard".

That same year, English geologist JOHN PHILLIPS came up with the first timescale of Earth based on the creatures found in rock fossils.

Fossilized finds

Anning found hundreds of fossils of **fascinating creatures that nobody knew existed** on the same coast, including the skeleton of the **world's first plesiosaur** (near-lizard) in 1821. Anning's discoveries led other scientists to realize that this coastline had formed **185 MILLION YEARS AGO**. Strong winds, rain, and waves had crumbled the rock layers away, helping Anning to uncover the fossils.

Anning's sketch of one of her findings – a *Plesiosaurus* fossil

Understanding evolution

Anning had been raised to believe that **God had created all living things**. However, her findings **challenged the traditional belief** that Earth's species had always existed unchanged. Her discoveries proved that different creatures had **LIVED, DIED OUT, AND EVOLVED** over time.

By the way...
I am said to be the inspiration for the famous tongue-twister, "She sells seashells by the seashore."

How she changed the world

Mary Anning did the dirty work, searching the sands so that palaeontologists (scientists who study fossils) could analyse her finds and develop new theories. Despite not having any formal education or training, she helped to change our view of how life evolved on Earth.

English scientist Charles Darwin wrote about the theory of evolution in his book **ON THE ORIGIN OF SPECIES** in 1859.

In 2001, Dorset's Jurassic Coast became a **UNESCO WORLD HERITAGE SITE**, 200 years after Mary Anning first explored there.

Sofia Kovalevskaya

The Russian SUPER-SCHOLAR who excelled at science and mathematics

Kovalevskaya's childhood home in Russia

Algebra addict

Sofia Kovalevskaya was born in Moscow, Russia, in 1850. At the time, **girls in Russia received little education**, but young Kovalevskaya became **HOOKED ON MATHEMATICS**. Her father ordered her to concentrate on other studies, but Kovalevskaya *secretly borrowed an algebra book* and read it at night!

Did you know?
My achievements include being the first woman to be elected to the Russian Academy of Sciences.

$$U_{xx} + U_{yy} = 0$$
$$U(x,0) = 0$$
$$U_y(x,0) = n^{-1}\sin nx$$

No women allowed

Kovalevskaya was **determined to go to university** – but women were not allowed to study in universities in Russia. Kovalevskaya persisted and, eventually, she got *special permission* to study in Germany. She became the first woman in Europe to be awarded a **DOCTORATE IN MATHEMATICS**.

Kovalevskaya studied the changing shape of Saturn's rings.

How she changed...
Kovalevskaya made some important breakthroughs in the world of mathematics, paving the way for other women to work in the academic world.

the world

Kovalevskaya made new discoveries about how objects such as tops spin.

A brilliant career

Kovalevskaya scored another first for women when she was made a **MATHS PROFESSOR** at the University of Stockholm, in Sweden. When she **won a major maths prize** at the *French Academy of Science* in 1888, they were so impressed by her work that they increased her prize money from 3,000 to 5,000 francs!

Star student

Lise Meitner was born into a Jewish family in Vienna, Austria, in 1878. Although there were **limited education opportunities for girls**, she excelled at science. When she got a job as a researcher for **PHYSICIST MAX PLANCK** she had to work on her own as *women were not allowed on university premises*.

Max Planck studied the behaviour of atoms.

Otto Hahn

Important discoveries

At the University of Berlin in Germany, Meitner and her **laboratory partner, Otto Hahn**, experimented with uranium. Meitner formed a theory that uranium atoms could be split in two, *releasing huge amounts of energy*. This process is called **NUCLEAR FISSION**.

Lise Meitner

The brilliant PHYSICIST who discovered the awesome power of nuclear energy

Nazis defaced Jewish-run shops in Germany as part of their campaign against Jews.

DREIFUSS & C°

Dramatic escape

In 1938, Meitner *fled to the USA to escape the Nazis'* murderous campaign against Jews in Germany, Austria, and elsewhere in Europe. After the war, her two **German colleagues took all the credit** – and a **NOBEL PRIZE** – for their work on nuclear fission. Meitner's contribution to physics has not been forgotten, however – element 109 was named Meitnerium in her honour.

How she changed...

At a time of great personal danger, Meitner's theories on nuclear fission laid the foundations for the development of nuclear energy.

the world

35

Marie Curie
RADIATION revolutionary

History's foremost female physicist was in her element pioneering ground-breaking advances in science and medicine.

Ray of hope

Curie proved that atoms of some elements release high-energy particles in a process called radiation. With Pierre, she **DISCOVERED TWO NEW ELEMENTS** – polonium (named after Poland, her home country) and radium (named after the Latin word for "ray"). They also **coined the term "radioactivity"**, and found that radiation could help *treat diseases such as cancer.*

Did you know?
Curie's research papers are radioactive, and are stored in protective lead-lined boxes.

Pierre Curie

Scientific schooling

Maria Salomea Skłodowska was born in Poland in 1867. She was *introduced to science by her parents*, who were both teachers. **A TALENTED STUDENT**, she moved to Paris, France, in 1891 to study **physics and mathematics**. She married French physicist Pierre Curie four years later.

Who came before...

German physicist **WILHELM ROENTGEN** discovered X-rays in 1895. The radioactive element roentgenium is named after him.

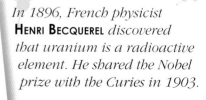

In 1896, French physicist **HENRI BECQUEREL** discovered that uranium is a radioactive element. He shared the Nobel prize with the Curies in 1903.

Double award

In 1903, Marie and Pierre won the *Nobel Prize in Physics.* Pierre died in a tragic accident three years later, and Marie took his teaching position, becoming the **first female professor** at the Sorbonne University in Paris. Her research led to **ANOTHER NOBEL PRIZE**, in Chemistry, in 1911.

By the way...
I was the first woman to win a Nobel Prize, and am the only person to win Nobel Prizes in multiple sciences.

Mobile X-ray unit in use during World War I

Wartime wounded

During World War I, Curie developed a smaller, mobile version of a hospital **X-RAY MACHINE** for ambulances to scan wounded soldiers in the field en route. *Years of being exposed to radiation* caused her death in 1934. The **Marie Curie organization** was set up in 1948 to care for terminally ill patients.

How she changed the world

At a time when science was a male domain, Curie did not let gender hold her back. She devoted her life to the subject and, despite paying the ultimate price for her radiation research, has improved the lives of millions.

Who came after...

New Zealand scientist **ERNEST RUTHERFORD** *revealed the structure of an atom and split it apart in the first demonstration of nuclear physics.*

Daughter of Marie and Pierre, **IRÈNE JOLIOT-CURIE** *followed in her parents' footsteps, winning the Nobel Prize in Chemistry in 1935.*

Healthcare heroes

The CAREGIVERS who stood out from the crowd

Women have always been involved in healthcare, but for a long time they were restricted to nursing. These days, female doctors are becoming increasingly common. These caregivers were pioneers in their fields.

Mary Seacole

When the **CRIMEAN WAR** broke out in 1853, Jamaican-Scottish nurse Mary Seacole volunteered to help but was rejected – possibly because of her **mixed-race heritage**. Undeterred, she travelled to Crimea (on the northern coast of the Black Sea) and built her "British Hotel" from abandoned wood, metal, and glass. Here, she *cared for soldiers*, and sometimes even tended to them on the battlefield itself.

Florence Nightingale

Horrified at the filthy conditions in which wounded soldiers were treated during the Crimean War, English social reformer Florence Nightingale and her team of nurses set about *cleaning the rat-infested wards* and improving efficiency in medical care. As a result, the number of patient deaths was dramatically reduced. After the war, Nightingale set up a **NURSE TRAINING SCHOOL** in London.

Edith Cavell

When **WORLD WAR I** broke out in 1914, Edith Cavell was already known for pioneering nursing work in Belgium. *She nursed the wounded from both sides of the conflict*, and risked her life to help Allied soldiers escape from German-occupied Belgium. She was **sentenced to death by firing squad** for her espionage.

Agnes Hunt

Despite suffering from a painful hip condition, Agnes Hunt *worked tirelessly to help physically disabled children*. She turned her home in Shrewsbury, UK, into a **CHILDREN'S CONVALESCENT HOME** in 1900. Hunt later teamed up with surgeon Robert Jones to found a large hospital and training facility specializing in **bone and joint disorders**.

Averil Mansfield

A role model to women trying to succeed in a male-dominated field, Averil Mansfield *pioneered stroke-preventing surgery* and, in 1993, became the **UK's first female professor of surgery**. Her diverse medical career has covered research and teaching, and she was president of the **BRITISH MEDICAL ASSOCIATION (BMA)** in 2009–2010.

Chien-Shiung Wu

The PHYSICS pioneer

Chien-Shiung Wu was a Chinese-American nuclear physicist who worked on creating the world's first atomic bomb.

Nanjing University, China, where Wu studied from 1930 to 1934

By the way...
Since relations between the USA and China were strained after China's communist revolution in 1949, I was unable to return to China until 1973.

Early life

Chien-Shiung Wu grew up in China and **studied maths and physics** at Nanjing University. In 1936, she headed to the USA to **STUDY RADIOACTIVITY**. Her supervisor, American Ernest Lawrence, had invented a new kind of particle accelerator. Wu used this to *split uranium atoms and produce radioactive isotopes* (versions of an element that have the same number of protons but different numbers of neutrons).

Who came before...

French scientist **IRÈNE JOLIOT-CURIE** *won the Nobel Prize in 1935 for discovering artificial radioactivity. She was the daughter of the physicists Marie and Pierre Curie.*

American physicist **J. ROBERT OPPENHEIMER** *directed the Manhattan Project and became known as "the father of the atomic bomb".*

The Manhattan Project

Wu finished her studies in 1940, but stayed in the USA to *research radioactivity* further. She became an **EXPERT** in her field, and was asked to join the top-secret Manhattan Project: the research project that created the **atomic bomb** that ended World War II.

The first nuclear weapon was tested in the New Mexico desert, USA, on 16 July 1945.

Beta decay

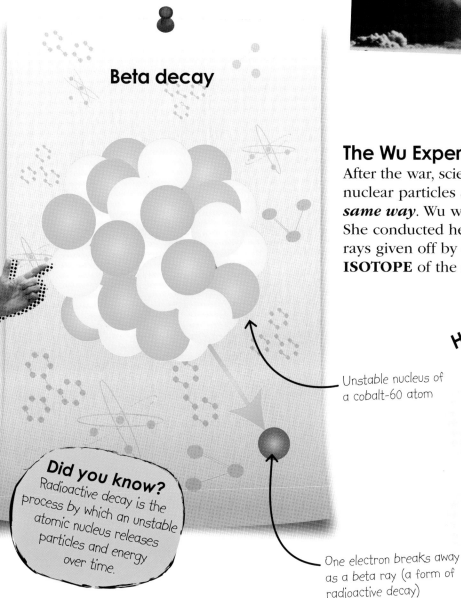

The Wu Experiment

After the war, scientists put forward the idea that nuclear particles *don't always decay in the same way*. Wu was the first to prove this theory. She conducted her **Wu Experiement** using beta rays given off by cobalt-60, a **RADIOACTIVE ISOTOPE** of the element cobalt.

Unstable nucleus of a cobalt-60 atom

How she changed the world

Wu made some incredible contributions to science, at an important time in history. Thanks to her example, many more women were encouraged to take up careers in science.

Did you know?

Radioactive decay is the process by which an unstable atomic nucleus releases particles and energy over time.

One electron breaks away as a beta ray (a form of radioactive decay)

Who came after...

MELISSA FRANKLIN *is a physicist at Harvard University in Massachusetts, USA. Her team found evidence of a particle known as the top quark in 1995.*

Italian physicist **FABIOLA GIANOTTI** *began her five-year post in charge of CERN (Conseil Européen pour la Recherche Nucléaire) – the top body in Europe for nuclear research – in 2016.*

Dian Fossey

The ZOOLOGIST who put mountain gorillas on the map

A change of career

Raised in California, USA, Dian Fossey began her career as **an occupational therapist**. While travelling in Africa in 1963 she *became interested in primates*. She was invited to study mountain gorillas, and soon established the **KARISOKE RESEARCH CENTER** in Rwanda.

By the way...
I wrote the memoir *Gorillas in the Mist*, which was later made into a major film starring American actor Sigourney Weaver.

Primate pals

The *mountain gorilla population was rapidly dwindling* in Rwanda due to poaching and loss of habitat. Fossey set out to **UNDERSTAND AND PROTECT** the remaining gorillas. To get close to them, **she imitated their behaviour**, scratching herself, beating her chest, and copying the gorillas' belch-like calls.

Fossey was buried next to her favourite gorilla, Digit, who was killed by poachers.

DIGIT 1965–1977

Mysterious murder

Fossey **spent 18 years studying** the structure and rituals of the gorillas' society. She was murdered in 1985, a crime that remains unsolved. Her **RESEARCH** is continued today through the *Dian Fossey Gorilla Fund International*.

How she changed...
Before Fossey's research, gorillas were not well understood. Her work has increased our knowledge, helping us to protect them.
the world

Killer virus

In the 1980s, the **deadly AIDS** (Acquired Immunodeficiency Syndrome) disease became a crisis after after it killed millions of people. French virologist Françoise Barré-Sinoussi conducted research on an infected patient and discovered that an aggressive virus, **HIV** (Human Immunodeficiency Virus) was *the cause of AIDS*.

Françoise Barré-Sinoussi

The VIROLOGIST who discovered the deadly HIV virus

— HIV virus

By the way...
Though we cannot currently cure HIV, my research has allowed sufferers to lead longer, healthier lives.

How she changed...
Barré-Sinoussi's work on the HIV virus has improved treatment for sufferers, and may one day lead to a cure for the illness.

the world

Fighting AIDS

Barré-Sinoussi **travelled to Africa and Asia** to find out more about AIDS. She also became active in humanitarian organizations *fighting the crisis*. She conducted vital laboratory research and co-authored many scientific publications. In 2008, she shared the **NOBEL PRIZE** in Medicine with virologists Luc Montagnier from France and Germany's Harald zur Hausen.

Rosalind Franklin

The brilliant chemist who helped unravel the SECRET OF LIFE

Rosalind Franklin played a crucial role in working out the structure of DNA, the chemical "instructions" contained in the cells of all living creatures.

> **By the way...**
> My father thought science was an unsuitable career for a woman and did his best to discourage me.

Pioneering scientist

Born in London, UK, in 1920, Franklin studied **natural sciences** at Cambridge University. At that time, scientists knew that a substance found in the nucleus of cells called deoxyribonucleic acid (DNA) carries information, but not how it does this. In 1951, Rosalind began studying the structure of DNA alongside scientist Maurice Wilkins at King's College, London. Using a special technique called ***X-ray diffraction***, Franklin produced a photograph – now known as "Photograph 51" – which suggested that DNA had a **DOUBLE-HELIX** structure.

Who came before...

The 19th-century Swiss scientist **JOHANNES FRIEDRICH MIESCHER** *was the first to identify "nuclein" – now called DNA. It would be another 75 years before its significance would be fully understood.*

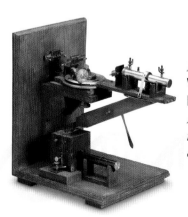

In 1915, father and son **WILLIAM AND LAWRENCE BRAGG** *won the Nobel Prize in Physics for their pioneering work on X-ray diffraction.*

The DNA race

Scientists **Francis Crick and James Watson** were also researching DNA. Without Franklin's permission, Wilkins showed "Photograph 51" to Watson. Crick and Watson combined this with their own research and published the results. They explained that the double-helix shape is made up of bases, which **ZIP** together. When the genetic information needs to be copied, the two sides of the double-helix unzip, each able to assemble new strands. They gave Franklin no *credit for her work*.

"Photograph 51" was a turning point in understanding DNA.

Francis Crick

Franklin studied the tobacco mosaic virus, which was the first virus ever isolated.

James Watson

The bases are made of four substances: adenine, thymine, cytosine, and guanine.

Virus research

Franklin went on to research the *structure of viruses*, and gave many talks on her findings. She **continued working until her death** from cancer in 1958. In 1962, Wilkins, Crick, and Watson were awarded the **NOBEL PRIZE** for their work on DNA.

How she changed the world

At a time when very few women followed a career in science, Franklin pursued her ambition to be a chemist with determination. The discovery of the structure of DNA was one of the 20th century's most important scientific advances, though she didn't receive the credit for her part in it during her lifetime.

What came after...

The study of DNA has revolutionized the field of **FORENSIC SCIENCE**. Everybody's DNA is different, so a criminal can be identified from the DNA that he or she leaves behind at a crime scene.

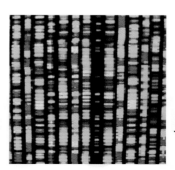

Completed in 2003, the **HUMAN GENOME PROJECT** studied human DNA to map all the genes of human beings. It found we have around 24,000 genes, only a few more than chimpanzees.

Inspiring campaigners

Society is transformed by women and men who stand up and make their voices heard. Throughout history, radical women have lit up campaign trails, actively pursuing their goals and stopping at nothing to achieve them. In the fight for justice, their struggles have challenged the treatment of women, religious groups, and ethnic minorities. These political and social activists have used everything from peaceful protests to all-out anarchy to right wrongs and make the world a better place.

Olympe de Gouges

The courageous POLITICAL ACTIVIST who fought for equality

Artists and writers attend a reading in a Paris salon.

A new life in Paris

Born in southwestern France in 1748, Olympe de Gouges **moved to Paris** when she was just 22. She was drawn to the **crowd of writers and artists** who met in the salons (drawing rooms) of well-to-do ladies. She soon began to write plays and pamphlets with a **POLITICAL MESSAGE**.

By the way...
My real name was Marie Gouze. My pen name, Olympe de Gouges, was a combination of my parents' names – Olympe Moisset and Pierre Gouze.

De Gouges's political writings led to her execution by guillotine in 1793.

How she changed...
De Gouges wrote the first manifesto for women's rights. English writer Mary Wollstonecraft wrote the second a year later.

the world

The Revolution

In 1789, the French, demanding liberty and equality, **overthrew their king**. De Gouges was for the Revolution until she realized **it overlooked women**. She wrote a document in 1791 called *The Declaration of the Rights of Woman and the Female Citizen*, which called for **EQUALITY** among the sexes.

Stanton studied at Troy Female Seminary.

Born reformer

American social activist Elizabeth Cady Stanton was born in 1815. She received a *full education*, which was unusual for girls at this time. Stanton became involved in the **temperance (anti-alcohol) and abolitionist (anti-slavery)** movements. In 1848, she wrote the *Declaration of Sentiments*, which argued for **WOMEN'S RIGHTS**.

By the way...
I was president of the National Woman Suffrage Association for 20 years.

How she changed...
Stanton's Declaration of Sentiments laid the foundations for American women finally winning the vote in 1920.
the world

Universal suffrage

The American Civil War (1861–1865) was won by the Union, but most only wanted the vote for black men, not women. Stanton **demanded universal suffrage** – allowing all men and women to vote. When the groups calling for the vote for women united as the *National American Woman Suffrage Association* in 1890, Stanton was elected its **PRESIDENT**.

Elizabeth Cady Stanton

The American activist who introduced WOMEN'S RIGHTS to the USA

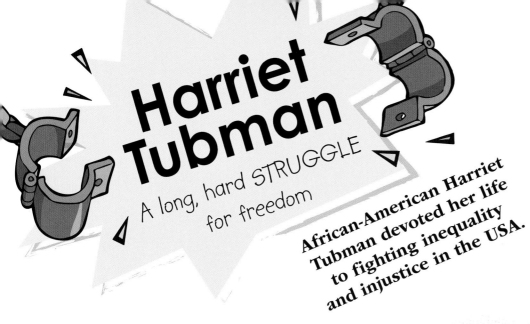

Harriet Tubman

A long, hard STRUGGLE for freedom

African-American Harriet Tubman devoted her life to fighting inequality and injustice in the USA.

Born a slave

Tubman was born a slave on a farm in Maryland, USA, around 1820. **Determined to escape**, she finally fled to Philadelphia, USA, a free state in which slavery was outlawed, in 1849. She travelled via a network of *secret routes and safe houses* used by anti-slavery activists, known as the **UNDERGROUND RAILROAD**.

Railroad to freedom

Once *Tubman was free*, she didn't forget the people she had left behind. She **risked her life** many times to **GUIDE HUNDREDS OF SLAVES** – including her own parents – from the southern slave states to the northern free states, and even to Canada.

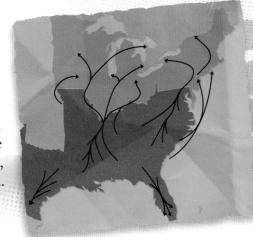

Free states

Slave states

➔ Underground Railroad routes

What came before...

*In 1619, the first ship containing **AFRICAN SLAVES** arrived in Jamestown, Virginia, USA. The slave trade had begun.*

*The slave trade was abolished in England in 1807, largely due to the campaigning of politician **WILLIAM WILBERFORCE**.*

Civil War hero

In 1861, **CIVIL WAR BROKE OUT** over slavery in the USA. Tubman served as a nurse and *spy for the Union*, who wanted to abolish slavery. She even led a successful military raid, guiding **300 troops** up the Combahee River in South Carolina to rescue up to 800 slaves.

The Combahee River was littered with mines, dropped by slave owners to deter raids like Tubman's.

Carry on campaigning

Slavery was finally abolished in the USA in 1865. Tubman opened a home for the elderly, and became a **PASSIONATE CAMPAIGNER** for *equal rights for African-Americans and votes for women*. She died, in the home she founded, at the age of 93.

How she changed the world

Although she was born into poverty and slavery, Tubman overcame all the odds to become one of the most important and effective campaigners against injustice in the history of the USA.

Did you know?
Tubman's nickname was "Moses" as, like the biblical figure, she led so many of her people to freedom.

What came after...

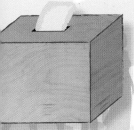

In 1920, seven years after Tubman's death, **WOMEN OVER THE AGE OF 21** in the USA were finally granted the right to vote.

An act guaranteeing all African-Americans the right to vote was signed into law by **US PRESIDENT LYNDON B. JOHNSON** in 1965 in the presence of African-American Civil Rights leader Martin Luther King, Jr.

Revolutionary fighter

Louise Michel worked as an ambulance nurse and **fought on the barricades against French troops** during the **PARIS COMMUNE** of 1871. The Commune was a revolutionary government that *took control of the city* after the country lost a war against Prussia. The French government tried to re-establish control, but failed, causing a stand-off.

Revolutionary workers defend the Paris Commune.

By the way...
In 1888, I survived an attempt on my life when a right-wing opponent shot me in the head.

Louise Michel

The REVOLUTIONARY who fought for a worker's government

The courtyard in front of the Basilica of the Sacred Heart, Paris, is named after Louise Michel.

Exile and return to Paris

After 72 days, the **Commune was crushed** by the French government. Michel was charged with attempting to overthrow the government. She was **EXILED** to the French islands of New Caledonia but pardoned seven years later. *Continuing to preach revolution*, Michel was imprisoned several times before her death aged 74.

How she changed...

Michel's heroism and devotion to her ideals made her one of the world's most celebrated female revolutionaries.

the world

Von Suttner's birthplace in Prague, Czech Republic

Bertha von Suttner

The novelist and PACIFIST who became the first woman to receive the Nobel Peace Prize

Aristocratic beginnings

Born Countess Kinsky in 1843, Bertha was working in Vienna, Austria, when she **fell in love with Baron Arthur von Suttner**. Facing family disapproval, she moved to Paris, France, and worked as a secretary for *Swedish inventor Alfred Nobel* for a short time. Returning to Vienna later, she and von Suttner **ELOPED** to Russia.

By the way...
I was the only woman admitted to the opening ceremony of the first Hague Peace Conference in 1899.

Von Suttner's novel *Lay Down Your Arms!*

Die Waffen nieder!
von Bertha von Suttner

How she changed...
Von Suttner was an early campaigner for peace and humanitarian issues, and many of her ideas influenced the United Nations.

the world

Pioneering pacifist

After seeing the dreadful consequences of the Russo-Turkish war, von Suttner wrote her **hugely successful anti-war novel** *Lay Down Your Arms!* Devoting her life to **PACIFISM**, she lectured and travelled widely. Before he died, Alfred Nobel left the majority of his wealth to a committee that would award prizes for excellence. Many believe his contact with von Suttner's work convinced him to include a *Nobel Prize for Peace*, which she won in 1905.

Landmark moments

MAKING CHANGES to protect our rights and our planet

These women made their names in different fields, but they share one thing – they all overturned outdated ideas by speaking out.

Princess Isabel of Brazil

Whenever the Emperor of Brazil, Pedro II, was busy abroad, his daughter Princess Isabel **RULED** on his behalf. She used her power in 1888 to sign the "Golden Law", which *ended slavery in Brazil*. Though popular with the people, the move angered the powerful slave owners, who, along with other groups unhappy with Pedro's rule, rose up to **depose the imperial family** the following year.

> **Did you know?**
> Isabel fled to France after the coup, and spent the last 30 years of her life there.

Helen Keller

Robbed of her ability to hear, see, and speak by a childhood illness, American Helen Keller developed the ability to communicate by *learning to sign, speak, lip-read, and use Braille*. She later became the **first deaf-blind person to gain a degree**. Keller went on to write 12 books and co-founded Helen Keller International, an organization that works around the world to **SAVE SIGHT**.

The word "hello" in Braille →

Rachel Carson

As a **marine biologist**, American Rachel Carson saw how chemicals affect the environment. Her 1962 book, *Silent Spring,* blamed a pesticide called DDT *for endangering birds and causing cancer in humans*. Carson's message gained much support from both the scientific community and the public. Shortly after her death in 1964, the US government set up its Environmental Protection Agency and **BANNED DDT**.

Wangari Maathai

In 1977, Professor Maathai founded Kenya's Green Belt Movement – an environmental organization dedicated to planting trees, conserving the environment, and women's rights. She believed **working with the land** was a way of improving both the environment and the lives of women. This annoyed big businesses, however, and Maathai was **ARRESTED MANY TIMES**. In 2002, she joined the government, and in 2004, she was the *first African woman to receive the Nobel Peace Prize*.

The Green Belt Movement has planted 51 million trees.

Margaret Chan

During the bird flu (1997) and SARS (2002) epidemics in southeast Asia, Chan was **Hong Kong's Director of Health**. Against fierce opposition, she *helped to control bird flu by culling 1.5 million chickens*. Chan headed the **WORLD HEALTH ORGANIZATION** (WHO) from 2006 to 2017.

Emmeline Pankhurst

The HERO who proved actions speak louder than words

Spearheading the campaign for women to get the vote in Britain, this leader made an impact on the lives of women worldwide.

Rebel with a cause

In 1858, **Emmeline Goulden** was born into a family of political activists. She *married Richard Pankhurst*, a supporter of women's equality. Later, she set up the **WOMEN'S FRANCHISE LEAGUE** to campaign for female suffrage (the right for women to vote).

Richard Pankhurst

Suffragette sisterhood

In 1903, Pankhurst set up the *Women's Social and Political Union* (WSPU) to fight for equality and the vote. A newspaper called the female members "**suffragettes**", and the name stuck. "**DEEDS, NOT WORDS**" was their motto, with suffragettes smashing windows and chaining themselves to railings to raise awareness of their cause.

Who came before...

In 1867, English politician JOHN STUART MILL *suggested women be allowed to vote. His idea was defeated in Parliament.*

In 1893, after a series of parliamentary petitions, NEW ZEALAND *became the first self-governing nation to grant women the right to vote.*

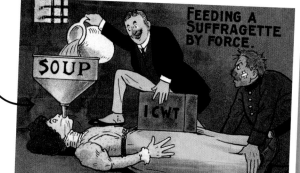

A cartoon showing a suffragette being force-fed to break her hunger strike

FEEDING A SUFFRAGETTE BY FORCE.

SOUP

ICWT

By the way...
My three daughters, Christabel, Sylvia, and Adela, were all very involved in the Suffrage Movement.

Hunger games

Many suffragettes were sent to prison, where they went on **hunger strike for their cause**. When World War I broke out in 1914, Pankhurst **CHANGED FOCUS**. She encouraged British women to take *jobs in factories and farms*, so men could fight on the front line.

A victory for voters

The suffragettes' tactics began to work. British women over 30 were given the **right to vote in 1918**. Women in the USA could vote by 1920, and other countries soon followed. Pankhurst *died in 1928,* shortly after British women were given the same voting rights as men, when the law changed so that **EVERYONE OVER 21 COULD VOTE**.

A woman casts her vote for the first time in 1918.

VOTES FOR WOMEN MEETING
Essex Hall Essex St Strand
ON MONDAY, NOV. 25

Did you know?
In 1987, Pankhurst's home opened as the Pankhurst Centre – a meeting place where women can learn and work together.

How she changed the world

Pankhurst led thousands of suffragettes to wage war against gender inequality, so that future generations of women could enjoy the same rights and freedoms as men.

What came after...

In the 1960s, the **WOMEN'S LIBERATION MOVEMENT** *fought for women to have equal status in society, with the same jobs and wages as men.*

In 2015, the **WORLD ECONOMIC FORUM** *predicted it might be another 118 years before the global pay gap between men and women is closed.*

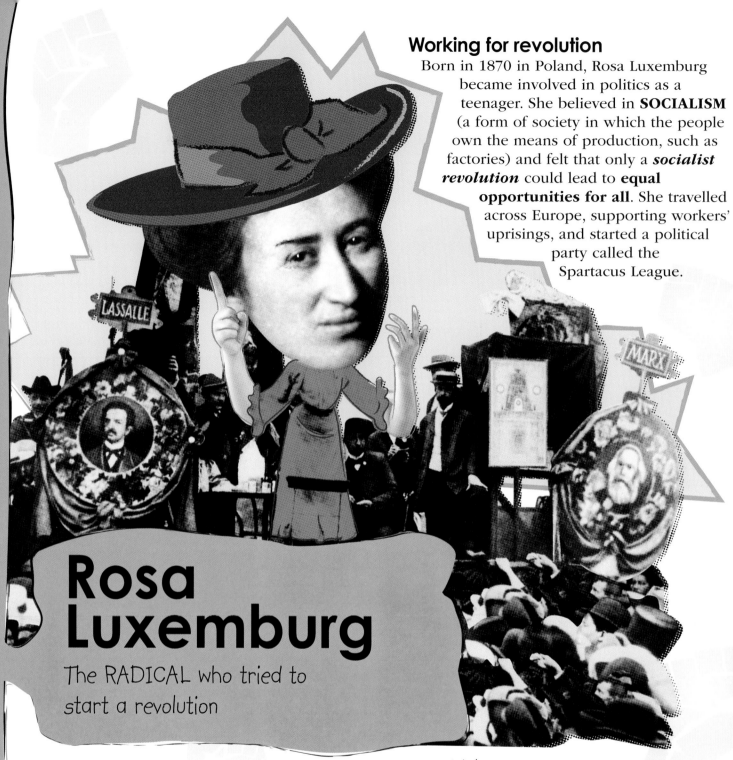

Working for revolution

Born in 1870 in Poland, Rosa Luxemburg became involved in politics as a teenager. She believed in **SOCIALISM** (a form of society in which the people own the means of production, such as factories) and felt that only a *socialist revolution* could lead to **equal opportunities for all**. She travelled across Europe, supporting workers' uprisings, and started a political party called the Spartacus League.

Rosa Luxemburg

The RADICAL who tried to start a revolution

How she changed...

Luxemburg lost her life fighting for the causes she believed in. Her fearless activism was an inspiration to many.

the world

A Spartacist is arrested during the crackdown in Germany.

Life cut short

The post-war German government was afraid that radicals such as Luxemburg were encouraging Germans to rise *against the government*. They began taking **TOUGH MEASURES**. In January 1919, Luxemburg was **captured** and shot dead, without even having a trial.

Growing up in Nazi Germany

German political activist Sophie Scholl was born in 1921. During her childhood, **Adolf Hitler** and the Nazi party came to power. Scholl and her brother Hans joined the *Hitler Youth Movement*, but they soon came to despise the **HATE-FILLED BELIEFS** of the Nazis.

Sophie Scholl

An ordinary student who STOOD UP to the might of Hitler and the Nazis

Resistance movement

As Germany fought against Britain and its allies in *World War II*, Scholl studied at the University of Munich. There, she and some other students formed the **WHITE ROSE** – a small, non-violent resistance movement that **carried out a pamphlet and graffiti campaign** against the Nazis.

The name "White Rose" signified innocence and purity.

A tragic end

Scholl, Hans, and another student, Christoph, were put on trial and **sentenced to death** for the "**CRIME**" of speaking up against Hitler. The brave students were executed the next morning. Witnesses later said that Scholl *remained calm and strong until the end*.

How she changed...

Decades after her death, Sophie is still a powerful symbol of bravery and resistance, both in Germany and worldwide.

the world

Rosa Parks

FIRST LADY of the Civil Rights Movement

This bus passenger found herself in the driving seat for Civil Rights at a time of racial intolerance. Her courage spurred the introduction of new laws that brought greater equality for all.

Divided society

Born in 1913, African-American Rosa Parks grew up at **a time of racial segregation** in the USA, with separate schools, social areas, and rules for black and white people. White children took a **BUS** to school, while black children often **had to walk**.

Blacks and whites are segregated during a social event in Alabama, USA.

Rebel's refusal

On 1 December 1955, Parks was travelling **HOME** by bus in Montgomery, Alabama, when the driver asked her to **give her seat to a white person**. She refused and the police **ARRESTED HER**.

What came before...

In 1954, the US Supreme Court ruled schools must offer **INTEGRATED EDUCATION** for all the nation's children.

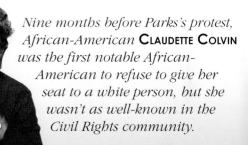

Nine months before Parks's protest, African-American **CLAUDETTE COLVIN** was the first notable African-American to refuse to give her seat to a white person, but she wasn't as well-known in the Civil Rights community.

Show of solidarity

Her arrest resulted in a *city-wide bus protest*, arranged by Civil Rights leader Dr Martin Luther King, Jr. Montgomery's **African-American community showed huge support for Parks** by staying at home or walking to work. After the city's buses went mostly empty for a year, **SEGREGATION ON BUSES WAS LIFTED** in 1956.

Rosa Parks marching from Selma to Montgomery

By the way...
I was given many awards, including the Martin Luther King, Jr. Award and the Presidential Medal of Freedom.

Later life

After the bus boycott, Parks **continued to fight for racial equality**. She took part in the marches from Selma, Alabama, to Montgomery in 1965 in protest against *restrictions on African-Americans voting*. She walked alongside Dr King. Parks continued to raise awareness of **INEQUALITY** until her death in 2005.

Did you know?
President Barack Obama said, "With the simplest of gestures, Parks helped change America and change the world."

How she changed the world

An understated act of defiance by Parks produced one of the defining moments of the Civil Rights Movement, proving that the actions of an individual can bring about positive change throughout society.

Who came after...

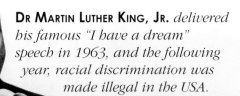

DR MARTIN LUTHER KING, JR. *delivered his famous "I have a dream" speech in 1963, and the following year, racial discrimination was made illegal in the USA.*

PRESIDENT BARACK OBAMA *made history in 2008 when he became the USA's first African-American president.*

Mary Robinson

The Irish legal expert who stood up for human rights.

This life-long campaigner used her powerful position to put human rights top of the political agenda.

Trinity College is Ireland's oldest university.

Did you know?
Mary Robinson is among the international leaders who make up The Elders, a global human rights organization founded by Nelson Mandela in 2007.

Legal eagle

Born in 1944 in the west of Ireland, Mary Robinson was always *tipped for the top*. She received a first-class education, studying at both Trinity College in Dublin and Harvard University in the USA. Academic success led this high flier to become Ireland's **youngest law professor** at the age of 25, as well as pursuing a career as a **BARRISTER**.

Who came before...

*The first UN High Commissioner for Human Rights – and Robinson's predecessor – was Ecuadorian ambassador **JOSÉ AYALA LASSO**, who held the post from 1994–1997.*

Who came after...

*The former President of Chile **MICHELLE BACHELET** is the current UN High Commissioner for Human Rights, in office since 2018.*

Pioneering president

A rapid rise to power saw Robinson take office as Ireland's **FIRST FEMALE PRESIDENT** in 1990. She proved to be a popular president, using her position to highlight the plight of people *at home and abroad*. She was the first international **head of state to visit** both war-torn Somalia and crisis-stricken Rwanda. She stepped down in 1997.

Robinson is greeted by women in Rwanda.

Caring campaigner

From 1997 to 2002, Robinson was the **United Nations (UN) High Commissioner for Human Rights**. While there, she publicized the plight of **refugees** and campaigned to end the death sentence for serious crimes in the USA. Today, Robinson champions new campaigns on climate change and **WOMEN'S RIGHTS**, in particular.

How she changed the world

Inspiring Ireland and the wider world, Mary Robinson has worked hard to break boundaries for women as both President of Ireland and in her work with the UN. She continues to draw attention to various injustices all over the world.

ESTHER IBANGA'S *Women Without Walls Initiative works towards empowering Nigerian women in all walks of life, regardless of ethnic, religious, or political background.*

ZAHRA' LANGHI *co-founded the Libyan Women's Platform for Peace, an organization that emphasizes women's rights, education, and political reform.*

Malala Yousafzai

A BRAVE voice speaking out for girls

By the way...
When I first began blogging, I used a fake name to protect my identity.

Even before she had reached her teens, Pakistani schoolgirl Malala Yousafzai had made a name for herself as a champion of education for girls.

Taliban trouble

In northwest Pakistan, the Taliban, a hardline religious terrorist group, had *banned girls from attending school*. In early 2009, aged only 11, Yousafzai began taking action by **writing a blog** to draw attention to this injustice. Her brave stance won praise and even a **NATIONAL YOUTH PEACE PRIZE**, but she also attracted the attention of the Taliban.

Who came before...

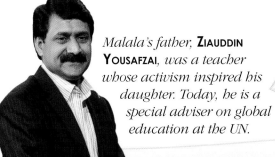

Welsh businesswoman **ANN COTTON** *started Camfed (Campaign for Female Education) in 1993. Its aim is to educate and empower young African women.*

Malala's father, **ZIAUDDIN YOUSAFZAI**, *was a teacher whose activism inspired his daughter. Today, he is a special adviser on global education at the UN.*

Attack

Although Yousafzai received **DEATH THREATS**, she carried on attending school. In October 2012, a Taliban gunman boarded her school bus and **shot her in the head**. Though she narrowly avoided death, one bullet *damaged her brain*. After initial treatment in Pakistan, she was flown to the UK for specialist treatment.

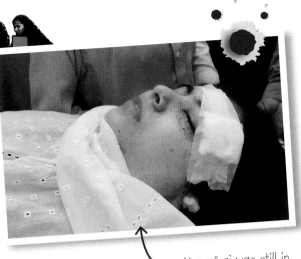

Yousafzai was still in a coma when she arrived in the UK.

Did you know...
The Malala Fund works across the world to win the right for every girl to have at least 12 years of quality education.

Yousafzai with her Nobel Peace Prize

How she changed the world

Thanks to Yousafzai's bravery and persistence, the UN has renewed its promise to fight for primary education for every child in the world. And, in her native Pakistan, every child now has the right to free education.

Aftermath

Within just months after the shooting, Yousafzai had made an **amazing recovery**. She attended school in the UK, gave a speech at the United Nations (UN) headquarters in New York, and *wrote her autobiography*. In 2014, she became the youngest person ever to win the **NOBEL PEACE PRIZE**.

Who came after...

In 2014, British actor **EMMA WATSON** *launched the UN's HeForShe campaign, which aims to get both women and men involved in gender equality issues.*

The Norwegian government, *led by Prime Minister* **ERNA SOLBERG**, *announced it would begin funding education initiatives in Africa from 2014.*

Leading

ladies

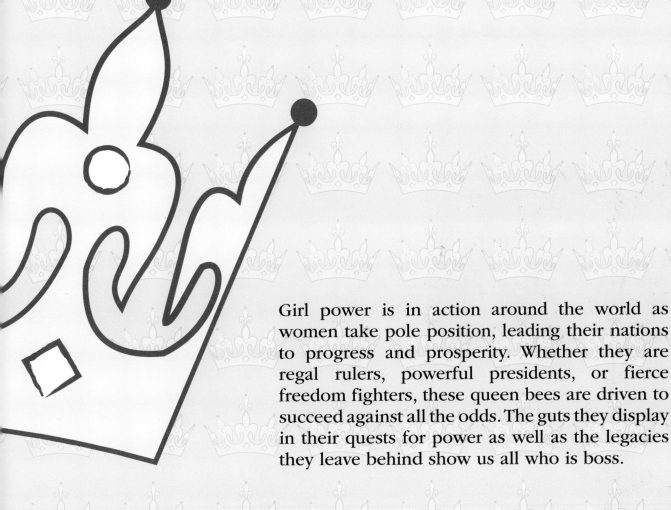

Girl power is in action around the world as women take pole position, leading their nations to progress and prosperity. Whether they are regal rulers, powerful presidents, or fierce freedom fighters, these queen bees are driven to succeed against all the odds. The guts they display in their quests for power as well as the legacies they leave behind show us all who is boss.

Joan of Arc

From farm girl to NATIONAL HERO

She led her nation's troops, broke a siege, helped a prince claim the throne, and was put to death – and all by her 20th birthday.

Mission from God

Joan was born into a peasant family in France in 1412. When she was 13, she believed **angels and saints spoke** to her, revealing **GOD'S PLAN** for her: Joan would help defeat the English in the Hundred Years' War and install Charles, heir to the French throne, as **King of France**. It took Joan a few years to work up the courage to tell Charles.

The Hundred Years' War between France and England actually lasted for 116 years.

Ready for battle

Joan rode for 11 days, through enemy territory, to reach Charles and tell him her mission. At first, he refused to take her seriously, but **Joan eventually won him over**. Royal craftsmen made Joan a *special suit of armour*. Joan was ready to **LEAD THE FRENCH ARMY INTO BATTLE**.

Who came before...

Joan's battles were part of the Hundred Years' War. It began when **KING EDWARD III OF ENGLAND** *attempted to seize the throne of France, declaring that he was the rightful king.*

England's most successful military commander in the war was Edward III's eldest son, Edward of Woodstock, nicknamed **THE BLACK PRINCE** *by the French.*

Maid of Orléans

The army was lifted by Joan's divine messages as they marched to the **CITY OF ORLÉANS**, which had been under siege by the English for six months. Within days, the confident French soldiers **broke the siege** and the English fled. Joan escorted Charles to the city of Reims, where he was crowned King of France in 1429. Joan's **holy mission was accomplished**.

By the way...
Two of my brothers, Jean and Pierre, fought alongside me at Orléans.

Bitter end

Almost a year later, Joan was **captured and handed over** to the English and found guilty of **DISOBEYING GOD'S LAWS**. On 30 May 1431, in the French town of Rouen, 10,000 people watched as Joan was **burned to death**.

How she changed the world

Joan's bravery and unshakeable belief in God's purpose for her has made her one of history's most powerful symbols of courage, patriotism, and faith.

What came after...

In 1453, the Hundred Years' War finally ended with a decisive victory for France at the **BATTLE OF CASTILLON**.

Almost 500 years after her death, **POPE BENEDICT XV** officially declared Joan a saint of the Catholic Church. Her feast day is 30 May – the anniversary of her death.

Cool queens

From feisty pharaohs to eminent EMPRESSES

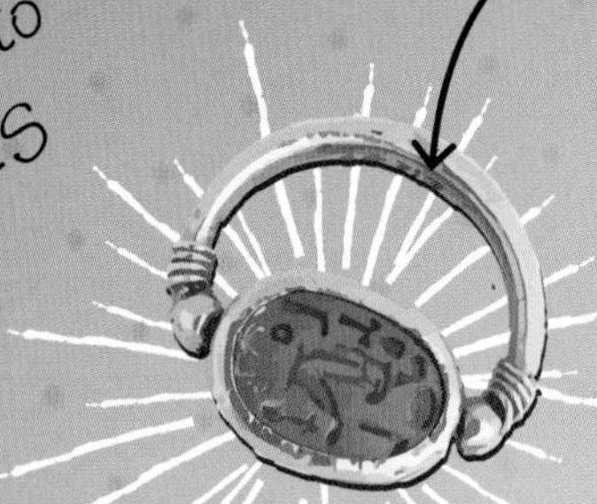

Throughout history, being a ruler was seen as mainly a man's job. But plenty of powerful women have shown that women can be as memorable monarchs as men.

Hatshepsut's cartouche – her name written in symbols called hieroglyphs – means "first among noble women".

Hatshepsut

Given charge in 1473 BCE when the new pharaoh was only a baby, Hatshepsut soon **declared herself pharaoh**, even **DRESSING** as a male ruler would. Historians rate Hatshepsut as one of Egypt's *most important pharaohs*.

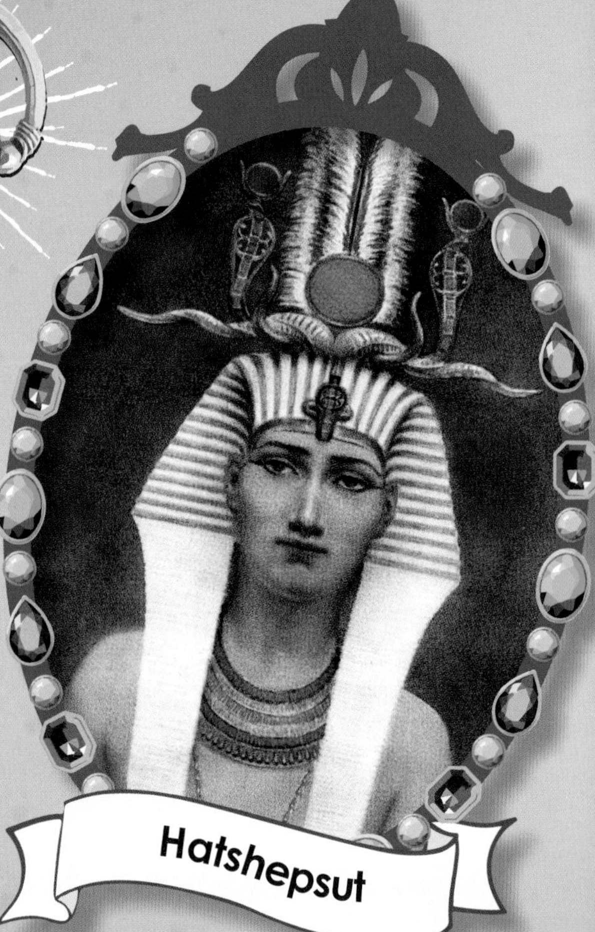

Hatshepsut

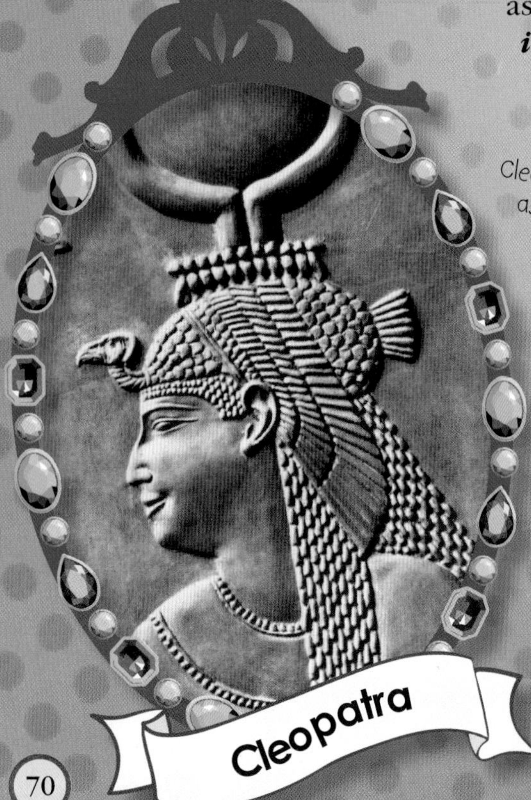

Cleopatra depicted herself as a reincarnation of the goddess Isis.

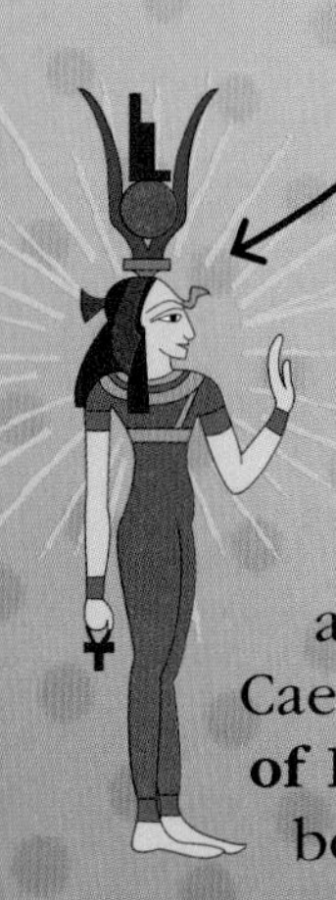

Cleopatra

Cleopatra was a **RUTHLESS, INTELLIGENT RULER**, who kept Egypt *safe from Roman invasion* by forming alliances with powerful Romans, such as Julius Caesar. She was eventually **defeated by the might of Rome**. She killed herself in 30 BCE and Egypt became part of the Roman Empire.

Cleopatra

70

Eleanor of Aquitaine

Eleanor was **one of the most powerful figures of the Middle Ages**, married to two kings and the mother of two more. ***As Queen of France, then England***, she helped her husbands to manage their realms. She then **RULED ENGLAND** while her son, King Richard I, fought in wars overseas.

Eleanor came from the richest family in France and had her own coat of arms.

Eleanor of Aquitaine

Razia Sultana

Razia al-Din was the **ONLY WOMAN RULER** of the Delhi Sultanate, a Muslim kingdom in the north of modern-day India. Her father didn't think much of his sons' abilities, so he ***named his daughter his heir*** instead. Razia **led her troops on the battlefield** and ruled for four years before being ousted in 1240 by nobles who refused to accept a woman leader.

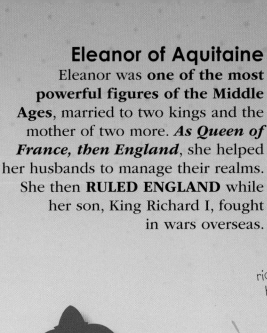

Razia Sultana

Named after the queen, the Victoria Cross is the highest award for bravery in the British armed forces.

Queen Victoria

As Queen of the United Kingdom from 1819, Victoria was also the **head of the vast British Empire**. At the Empire's height, Victoria reigned over **450 MILLION SUBJECTS**, almost a quarter of the planet's population. She ruled for more than 63 years, during an era of growing ***economic prosperity*** and industrialization.

Queen Victoria

Catherine the Great

This daughter of a German prince led Russia out of the past and into the future.

Russia's LONGEST-SERVING female ruler

From Russia with love

Sophie Auguste Friedericke von Anhalt-Zerbst-Dornburg was born in Germany in 1729. At the age of 15, she was **invited to Russia** by the Empress Elizabeth to meet – and perhaps marry – **GRAND DUKE PETER**, who was Elizabeth's son and **heir to the throne**.

Grand Duke Peter

Crowning moment

Grand Duke Peter and Sophie married in 1745, with the bride taking the name Catherine. Shortly after **Peter became Tsar** (emperor) in 1762, Catherine became involved in a conspiracy against him, and had her husband **overthrown and arrested**. On 12 September 1762, Catherine was crowned **EMPRESS OF RUSSIA**. Her glorious reign lasted three decades.

Who came before...

In the 6th century, **EMPRESS THEODORA** transformed the Byzantine Empire with her political influence and ground-breaking reforms to improve life for women.

French queen **CATHERINE DE' MEDICI** was a powerful 16th-century leader, taking charge during the Wars of Religion. Three of her sons became kings of France.

Time for change

Introducing change and reform, Catherine extended the boundaries of Russia, improved the system of governing the provinces, and founded schools. She was also a great **patron of the arts** and developed and promoted the capital St Petersburg as a **CULTURAL CENTRE** of excellence.

Catherine ordered the construction of the Hermitage Theatre in St Petersburg. It showed plays and operas.

By the way...
I was an avid art collector, and the paintings, sculptures, and other treasures I amassed now form the basis of the Hermitage Museum in St Petersburg.

Denis Diderot

Enlightened empress

Catherine was also at the forefront of the **ENLIGHTENMENT** – a movement during which advances in science, politics, and philosophy changed the way many thought about the world. Philosophers such as Frenchmen **Diderot and Voltaire** corresponded with Catherine often, and she also **wrote many books herself**. After 34 years of rule, she suffered a stroke in 1796 and died.

Did you know?
Catherine was buried in an ornate coffin covered in expensive gold fabric.

How she changed the world

Catherine the Great heralded a Golden Age for Russia, bringing sweeping changes to a long-troubled nation. Driven by ambition and desire for progress, she modernized the country by pursuing goals of expansion, education, and enlightenment.

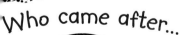

Who came after...

*In the 18th century, **Maria Theresa** of Austria was Holy Roman Empress and Queen of Hungary and Bohemia for 40 years. She reformed the national government and military.*

Queen Victoria *ruled Great Britain for 63 years, making monumental changes in government policy and hugely expanding the British Empire.*

Wu Zetian

The ONLY FEMALE ever to rule China

Rise to rule

Born in Bingzhou, China, in 624 CE, Wu Zetian **learned about running a country** when she was consort (second wife) to Emperor Taizong. After his death, Emperor Gaozong made her his consort, but Zetian soon began pulling the strings behind the scenes, **GAINING POWER** and making allies. After Gaozong's death in 690 CE, Zetian became the *Empress of China*.

Zetian had striking Buddhist statues carved into the Longmen Grottoes in China.

By the way... Under my rule, the famous trade route called the Silk Road opened, allowing new trading opportunities for China.

Golden era

During the **15 years of her rule**, Zetian introduced **POSITIVE CHANGES**: she developed the education system and improved farming techniques. *She recruited people based on ability rather than status*, and worked at maintaining foreign relations. She remained Empress until 705 CE, when some enemies within her court had her removed from power. She died shortly afterwards.

How she changed...

Fierce ambition ensured Zetian became Empress of China, with the country enjoying prosperity and peace under her rule.

the world

Formidable union

Born into an aristocratic family, Taytu Betul found happiness in her marriage to King Sahle Maryam of Shewa, a region of Ethiopia. *She helped found Addis Ababa*, which became the capital of Ethiopia in 1886. The king became Emperor Menelik II in 1889, so Betul **took the title of Empress**. When Italy attempted to colonize Ethiopia, Betul convinced Menelik to **DECLARE WAR**.

Ménélik

King Menelik II on horseback

By the way...
During the battle with Italy, my spies brought me critical information, giving Ethiopia an edge in the war.

Military mastermind

With the first Italo-Ethiopian War underway, the **BATTLE OF ADWA** of 1896 proved a turning point. *Betul was on the frontline leading her own battalion* as Ethiopia triumphed over Italy. The defeat of the Europeans served as a warning against colonizing Africa. Betul later **focused on trade links and modernization for her country**.

How she changed...
Empress Taytu Betul's heart was set on avoiding the European colonization of Ethiopia, and her military strategies helped protect her nation.
the world

Italian battalion

Ethiopian troops

Taytu Betul

The GREAT EMPRESS who led her nation to victory in the Battle of Adwa

Queen Elizabeth I

She defied the age to rule with power, STRENGTH, and intelligence

Perhaps the greatest of all English monarchs, this queen's remarkable 44-year reign saw the emergence of England as a world power.

Did you know?
Despite Elizabeth's long battle to overthrow her rival, Mary, Queen of Scots, she never met her.

Turbulent childhood

King Henry VIII with Elizabeth's mother, Anne Boleyn

Elizabeth was just **two years old** when her father, King Henry VIII, had her mother executed in 1536 after she failed to produce a male heir. Elizabeth and her older half-sister Mary were *exiled from the royal court*, but were eventually brought back into the line of succession. Elizabeth **BECAME QUEEN** after Mary's death in 1558.

The Golden Age

Following the persecution of Protestants during the reign of her Catholic half-sister, Mary I, Elizabeth worked to **RESTORE RELIGIOUS STABILITY**. Foreign trade flourished, and explorers such as Sir Francis Drake sought out new territory for England abroad. Elizabeth's reign was also a *period of great cultural achievement*, seeing the emergence of outstanding artists such as English playwright **William Shakespeare**.

Who influenced her...

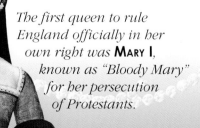

The first queen to rule England officially in her own right was **MARY I**, known as "Bloody Mary" for her persecution of Protestants.

WILLIAM CECIL *was Elizabeth's most trusted adviser, and one of the few people who remained a constant figure through most of her life.*

Bitter rivalry

Perhaps Elizabeth's greatest challenge was her **RIVALRY** with her cousin Mary, Queen of Scots. *With a claim to the English throne*, Mary was at the centre of plots to overthrow Elizabeth. In 1587, **Elizabeth made the difficult decision to have Mary killed.**

Death warrant of Mary, Queen of Scots

By the way...
I loved finery, and many women copied my style. When my teeth began to decay, some even blackened their teeth to match me!

The Spanish Armada

The defeat of the "invincible" Spanish Armada in 1588 was possibly *Elizabeth's finest hour*. King Philip II of Spain sent a fleet of 130 ships to the English Channel, with the aim of invading England. **Despite being greatly outnumbered**, the English navy – helped by bad weather – destroyed the Armada and emerged **VICTORIOUS**.

How she changed the world

A clever politician, Elizabeth was not afraid to be bold, and ushered in an age of peace and prosperity. Choosing to remain unmarried, her extraordinary success was all her own doing.

What came after...

Elizabeth's reign set the scene for the **GROWTH OF THE BRITISH EMPIRE**. *At its height, it controlled approximately one quarter of the world's land.*

Elizabeth's namesake, **QUEEN ELIZABETH II**, *is Britain's longest-reigning monarch. Today, the monarch has little political power, but upholds important traditions.*

Sacagawea

EXPLORER, guide, interpreter, and peacekeeper

A Native American from the Shoshone tribe, Sacagawea was a key member of a daring expedition into the American Wild West.

The Hidatsa lived in an area that is now North Dakota, USA.

Did you know?
Most of what we know about Sacagawea comes from Lewis's and Clark's journals about the trip.

Kidnapped!

Sacagawea, the *daughter of a chief of the Shoshone tribe*, was born in about 1788. When she was 12, she was **CAPTURED BY THE HIDATSA**, a rival tribe, and taken east to their homeland. A few years later, a Canadian fur trapper **made Sacagawea his wife**.

Go west

Sacagawea met American explorers **Meriwether Lewis and William Clark** in 1804, when they were exploring the American West. Sacagawea, with her husband and baby in tow, joined the expedition as an *interpreter and guide*. She also kept the party safe – the sight of her carrying her son reassured Native Americans, who **WELCOMED THE EXPLORERS** instead of attacking them.

Who came before...

ANCESTORS OF SACAGAWEA'S TRIBE *had lived in the American West since about 500 CE, as seen in ancient Shoshone artwork found in the region. Europeans arrived on the scene much later.*

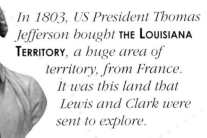

In 1803, US President Thomas Jefferson bought THE LOUISIANA TERRITORY, a huge area of territory, from France. It was this land that Lewis and Clark were sent to explore.

By the way...
During the journey I was amazed to bump into my brother, who I hadn't seen since I was kidnapped. He had become a Shoshone chief!

Sacagawea was celebrated on the US dollar coin in 2000.

Short life
After **seven months** and thousands of kilometres, the explorers finally reached their goal – the **PACIFIC OCEAN**. It is thought that Sacagawea died a few years later, **aged only 25**, and that Clark cared for her two children.

Meriwether Lewis

William Clark

Sacagawea was a key member of an expedition that changed the USA forever. It paved the way for settlement of The West, allowing the new country to expand and grow richer, until it became the world's wealthiest and most powerful nation.

How she changed the world

What came after...

In 1869, the first **COAST-TO-COAST RAILWAY** line was completed, triggering a boom in population and prosperity in The West.

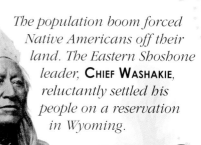

The population boom forced Native Americans off their land. The Eastern Shoshone leader, **CHIEF WASHAKIE**, reluctantly settled his people on a reservation in Wyoming.

79

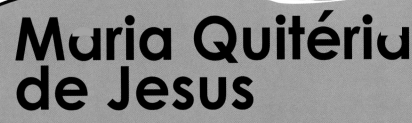

Maria Quitéria de Jesus

Brazil's BRAVEST HERO was a fearless fighter in the war for Brazilian independence

By the way...
In 1953, a century after my death, I was given the great honour of being named patron of the Brazilian Army.

Battle born

Maria Quitéria de Jesus was **RAISED ON HER FATHER'S FARM** in Bahia, Brazil, where she hunted, rode horses, and practised using weapons. This upbringing equipped her to serve in the *Brazilian War of Independence* (1822–1824). Fighting Portuguese domination, Maria was known for her **bravery and skill** in leading ambushes of the more numerous Portuguese soldiers.

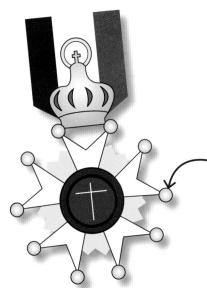

Imperial Order of the Southern Cross, awarded to Maria

Military honours

Maria was **PROMOTED TO CADET** and then to lieutenant in 1823. She was awarded the prestigious **Imperial Order** for her military service. In 1825, Portugal and Britain signed a treaty giving *Brazil the independence Maria had fought for*.

How she changed...
Maria's exceptional courage in conflict saw her play a major role in the struggle for Brazilian independence.

the world

A way with words

From a young age, Dolores Ibárruri wondered why there always seemed to be people who were **POOR**, while others were rich. She began speaking and writing about her ideas under the pseudonym "**La Pasionara**" (The Passion Flower). In 1920, she joined the **Spanish Communist Party**, which stated that all property should be owned by the people, and each person should share and benefit according to his or her needs.

By the way...
While in exile in the USSR, I was awarded the prestigious Lenin Peace Prize and the Order of Lenin.

A 1937 "Win the War" poster for the Communist party

Logo of the Partido Comunista de España (PCE) – Spain's Communist Party

Battle cry

In 1936, the **SPANISH CIVIL WAR** broke out. Ibárruri's strong speeches rallied the troops on the Republican (pro-communist) side, with her slogan "**¡No pasarán!**" (They shall not pass!). After the Republicans were defeated, *she was exiled* to the communist Soviet Union, and stayed there until 1977. When she returned to Spain, she became a member of parliament. She continued to speak out about communism until her death in 1989.

How she changed...
In male-dominated war-time, Dolores Ibárruri made her voice heard above all the others and earned her place as a revolutionary leader.

the world

Dolores Ibárruri
The Spanish "PASSION FLOWER" who strove for a fairer society

Eleanor Roosevelt

First Lady of the WORLD

Not content to take a back seat during her husband's presidency, Eleanor Roosevelt became a tireless campaigner for human rights.

Roosevelt at Allenswood Academy

Broken childhood

Born into a wealthy family in 1884, Eleanor became an **ORPHAN** at 10 years old. At the age of 15, she was sent to **Allenswood Academy**, near London, England, where the *feminist head teacher* encouraged the young student to think for herself.

Outspoken First Lady

Eleanor married **Franklin Roosevelt** in 1905. When he became president in 1933, she *dramatically reshaped the role of First Lady*, giving press conferences, and speaking in support of civil rights, young people's issues, and women's causes. She even wrote her own **NEWSPAPER COLUMN**, called "My Day".

What came before...

*The **MAGNA CARTA**, signed by King John of England in 1215, was a crucial turning point in the history of human rights.*

*The idea of human rights came to the fore during the 18th century, and was at the heart of the **AMERICAN AND FRENCH REVOLUTIONS**.*

Human rights

Eleanor became the first chairperson of the *United Nations Commission on Human Rights* in 1946. Two years later, she was the driving force behind the creation of the **UNIVERSAL DECLARATION OF HUMAN RIGHTS**, which states that everyone is entitled to the **same rights and freedoms**. Eleanor regarded this effort as her greatest achievement.

Eleanor with President John F. Kennedy in 1960

By the way...
I banned male reporters from my press conferences, forcing newspapers to employ female staff.

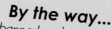

Universal Declaration of Human Rights

Final years

Eleanor *continued to champion many causes*, and, at the request of **President Kennedy**, she headed a **COMMISSION ON THE STATUS OF WOMEN**. Until her death at the age of 78, she continued to write her newspaper column, made television and radio broadcasts, and wrote many books.

How she changed the world

Through her dedication to many issues, Eleanor Roosevelt redefined the role of First Lady and effectively became a leader in her own right. She was called the "First Lady of the World" for her contribution to humanitarian causes, and remains an inspiration to millions.

What came after...

In 1963, the **MARCH ON WASHINGTON** *and Martin Luther King, Jr.'s stirring speech made the Civil Rights Movement something that politicians could no longer ignore.*

*The work of First Ladies such as Jacqueline Kennedy and **MICHELLE OBAMA** has been guided by Eleanor Roosevelt's example.*

Indira Gandhi

India's own IRON LADY

Independence struggle

The only child of Indian political leader Jawaharlal Nehru and his wife Kamala, Indira was born in 1917. While her father campaigned for **INDEPENDENCE FROM BRITISH RULE** under **the banner of the Indian Congress Party**, Indira involved local children in the fight with *posters and demonstrations*. After home tutoring, she attended European boarding schools, and married Feroze Gandhi in 1942.

Indians lie down on the streets of Delhi, India, to resist British rule.

The State Emblem of India

Prime Minister Jawaharlal Nehru

Father's footsteps

India gained independence in 1947, with Nehru appointed the nation's first prime minister. Gandhi worked with him before becoming **Congress Party President**. When her father and his replacement died in quick succession, the Congress Party made Gandhi **PRIME MINISTER IN 1966**.

Did you know...
Gandhi was friends with British Prime Minister Margaret Thatcher, and they admired each other's leadership.

Who came before...

Leader of the Indian independence movement **MOHANDAS GANDHI** *promoted peaceful demonstrations and protests against the British Empire.*

SIRIMAVO BANDARANAIKE *became the world's first female prime minister when she was elected leader of the Sri Lankan government in 1960.*

Political powerhouse

Gandhi introduced reforms aimed at **making India self-sufficient** in food production. This **GREEN REVOLUTION** was a success, and made food and jobs more plentiful. When a war broke out between the neighbouring eastern and western parts of Pakistan in 1971, Gandhi supported East Pakistan. India's involvement proved decisive, and East Pakistan broke away and *became Bangladesh*.

Rajiv Gandhi

By the way...
I served as Minister of Information and Broadcasting before becoming prime minister of India.

End of an era

Gandhi served three terms before being voted out. She led a **NEW CONGRESS PARTY** and was *re-elected to her fourth term* as prime minister in 1980. Four years later, Gandhi was assassinated by her bodyguards, who disagreed with some of her actions. Gandhi's **son Rajiv replaced** her as prime minister.

How she changed the world

India's first female prime minister turned the nation on its head, bringing opportunities, food, and jobs to its poorest people. Without her support, the newly independent country of Bangladesh would never have existed.

Who came after...

KHALEDA ZIA *became the first female prime minister of Bangladesh in 1991. She governed during a time of economic instability in the country.*

In 2014, India's annual **FOOD GRAIN PRODUCTION** *reached 250 million tonnes, compared to under 50 million tonnes in 1947.*

Margaret Thatcher

Britain's first FEMALE PRIME MINISTER

By the way...
I was lucky to escape with my life when a terrorist bomb exploded at the Conservative Party conference in 1984.

Iron Lady

Originally a research chemist, and then a barrister, Margaret Thatcher became a Conservative member of parliament (MP) in 1959. **Elected party leader**, she **BECAME PRIME MINISTER IN 1979**. Renowned for taking a tough stance on many issues, she set about reducing the power of the *trade unions* and raising taxes.

How she changed...

Thatcher's policies transformed the face of Britain, with some of her ideas – such as reducing the power of the unions – having lasting effects.

the world

British troops round up captured Argentinian soldiers.

Loved and loathed

Perhaps Thatcher's **BIGGEST SUCCESS** came in war. The Falkland Islands are an island chain off the coast of Argentina, but they are a British territory. When Argentina invaded in 1982, Thatcher ordered the British army to attack, **eventually regaining the islands**. She *divided opinion* up until her resignation in 1990. Some say she rescued Britain from economic decline, while others believe her tough policies ruined the livelihoods of millions.

Quiet beginnings

Born in West Germany in 1954, Angela Merkel began her **working life as a chemist** and *did not become politically active* until she was 36. When Germany was reunited in 1989, Merkel became a **SPOKESWOMAN** for **democracy**.

West Germans gather as East German soldiers break down a part of the Berlin Wall.

By the way...
At the end of the 1970s, I was asked to spy for the Stasi, or East German Secret Police. I declined.

Angela Merkel

Germany's first female CHANCELLOR

Rise to power

Joining the Christian Democratic Union (CDU) shortly before the reunification of Germany, Merkel soon became **Minister for Children and Youth**. She was elected leader of the party in 2000, and in 2005, became not only Germany's *first female chancellor* (head of the German government), but also its **YOUNGEST**.

Migrants crossing the Greece-Macedonia border

Mutti

Over three terms, Merkel has steered Germany through **MANY CRISES**. Perhaps the most notable was the 2011 *Syrian refugee crisis*, when she agreed to accept around 300,000 people fleeing civil war in Syria. Her steadfast approach earned her the nickname "**Mutti**", or "mother".

How she changed...
As a woman and a scientist, Merkel rose from political obscurity to lead Europe's richest economy.

the world

Political pioneers

Using POLITICS to make their points

These trailblazers helped to lead their countries, fight corruption, and campaign for human rights.

Golda Meir

Born in Russia in 1898, Golda Meir escaped the **anti-Jewish pogroms** (massacres and riots) at the age of eight. She believed that the Jewish people needed their own nation, and helped found the *Jewish state of Israel* in 1948. She later served as its **PRIME MINISTER** from 1969 to 1974.

Ellen Johnson Sirleaf

This gifted economist was a *finance minister* in her native Liberia until an army coup in 1980. Civil war and general unrest followed. When democracy returned, Sirleaf became Africa's first elected female head of state when she was made **Liberia's president** in 2006. She was awarded the **NOBEL PEACE PRIZE** in 2011 for fighting corruption.

Did you know?
More than two million Jews left Russia between 1880 and 1920 because of the pogroms.

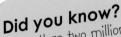

Iran's first female judge Shirin Ebadi was dismissed after the **IRANIAN REVOLUTION** in 1979 as the new government ruled that women should not hold high office. Undeterred, Ebadi began *legally defending* people who opposed the regime. She took an interest in human rights issues, especially the rights of women and children. Her work earned her the **Nobel Peace Prize**.

Graça Machel

Passionate about improving the standard of life for women and children, Graça Machel is a *politician and humanitarian* from Mozambique. She belongs to **THE ELDERS**, a group of **leaders from across the world** who work together to help solve serious problems, such as war, poverty, and climate change.

Benazir Bhutto

Born into a powerful political family, Benazir Bhutto became leader of the **Pakistan People's Party** (PPP) in 1982. The PPP campaigns for equality and social justice. Bhutto *twice served as prime minister* and was campaigning for a third term in office when she was **ASSASSINATED** in 2007.

Bhutto was Pakistan's first female prime minister when she took office in 1988.

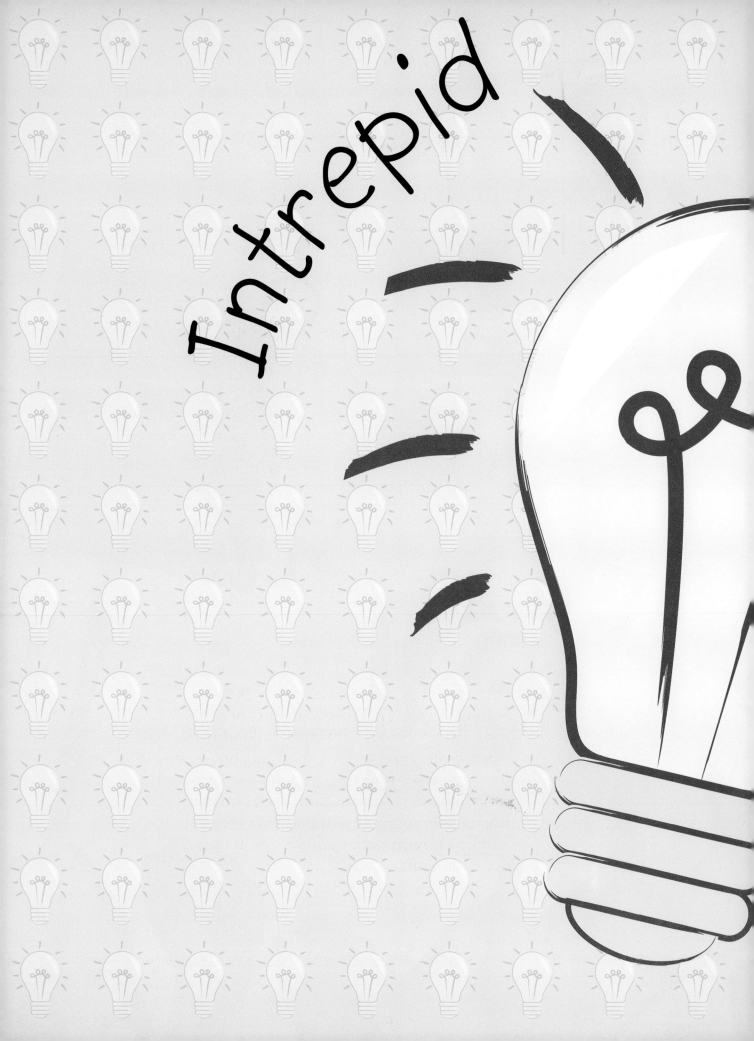

Intrepid

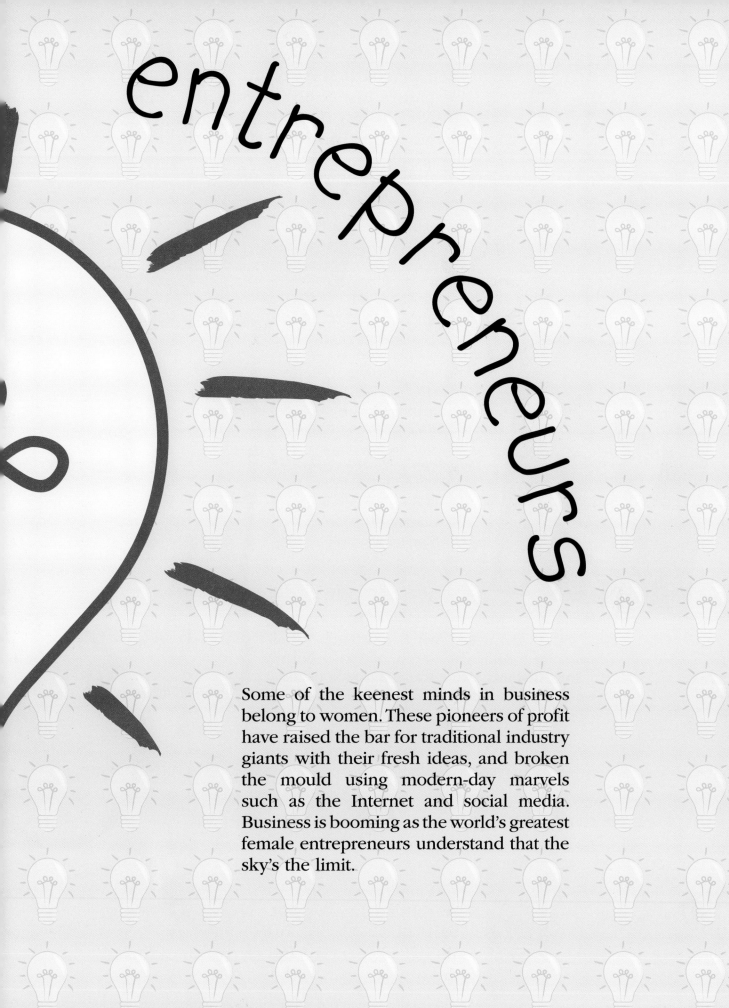

entrepreneurs

Some of the keenest minds in business belong to women. These pioneers of profit have raised the bar for traditional industry giants with their fresh ideas, and broken the mould using modern-day marvels such as the Internet and social media. Business is booming as the world's greatest female entrepreneurs understand that the sky's the limit.

Bertha Benz

Took the world's first ROAD TRIP

When Bertha Benz went for a spin in her husband's invention in 1888, she made history. It was the first long-distance drive in one of the world's earliest cars!

Did you know?
In 2008, the Bertha Benz Memorial Route opened, following the path of Bertha's historic trip.

Creative Karl

Bertha was the wife and business partner of German engineer **Karl Benz**. In 1885, Karl **BUILT HIS FIRST CAR**, but three years later, he was still *tinkering with the design*. Worried about losing out to competition, Bertha decided it was time to go public with Karl's invention.

Bertha's older son, Eugen, was 15 years old when he rode in the car.

The tyres were made of solid rubber, which meant a bumpy ride!

On the road

In August 1888, Bertha and her sons, Eugen and Richard, set off on the **world's first long-distance drive**, to demonstrate the car's capability. The destination was *Bertha's mother's house*, about 104 km (65 miles) away. As they motored along, the travellers attracted **LOTS OF ATTENTION**.

What came after...

The **FIRST KNOWN RACING EVENT** *was held in France in 1894, when 21 cars raced 127 km (79 miles) from Paris to Rouen.*

Motoring got more comfortable in 1902, when British engineer Edgar Hooley invented **TARMAC**. *The smooth, tough road surface was perfect for cars.*

Logo for Benz & Cie., Karl Benz's company

By the way...
The car's engine and two gears couldn't cope with steep hills, so my sons sometimes had to get out and push.

Richard, aged 13 at the time, was Bertha's younger son.

Mission accomplished

During the **12-hour trip**, Bertha made repairs to the car herself, including unblocking a fuel line with her hat pin. Her feat led to **BOOMING SALES** and, within 10 years, Karl Benz was running the *world's biggest motor company*.

How she changed the world

Bertha put cars on the map by showing the world what they were capable of. Her daring stunt brought worldwide attention to her husband's invention and brought their business stunning success.

American Mary Anderson played an important role in the history of road safety – she invented the **WINDSCREEN WIPER** in 1903.

The most successful female Formula 1 racer is Italian **LELLA LOMBARDI**, who came sixth in the 1975 Spanish Grand Prix.

Sarah Breedlove

America's first female SELF-MADE millionaire

An extraordinary businesswoman, Sarah Breedlove developed hair products, rising from a background of crippling poverty to take her place among America's elite entrepreneurs.

Did you know?
Many African-American women struggled at the time with hair loss due to poor nutrition and harsh soaps.

African-American washerwomen in the late 19th century

Harsh beginnings

Born to **former slaves** in 1867, Breedlove was the first child in her family to be born into **FREEDOM**. Married at 14 but widowed at 20, *she worked as a washerwoman*, earning just $1.50 a day. Breedlove began developing treatments after suffering hair loss.

The Walker Method

Breedlove **created a treatment** and advertised it with the help of her second husband, salesman Charles J. Walker. *She changed her name to Madam C. J. Walker* and travelled to promote the treatment, which she called the **"WALKER METHOD"**. This involved a special shampoo, scented oil that she said helped the hair to grow, and heated combs.

Who came before...

A former slave, African-American **CLARA BROWN** *set up a laundry business during the Colorado gold rush in the 19th century and used her earnings to help other freed slaves.*

African-American entrepreneur **ANNIE TURNBO MALONE** *was an important influence on Breedlove. The two later became fierce business rivals.*

Rise to the top

Breedlove's business became a **WILD SUCCESS**, and she began scaling up her operations. She opened factories, hair salons, and ***beauty schools to train her sales agents***. Many of the top roles in her business were filled by women. As sales rocketed, **she expanded her business internationally**.

Breedlove driving her electric car

By the way...
When I started my business, I was practically illiterate. Once I could afford to, I hired tutors to teach me to read and write.

Madam C. J. Walker's hair care product was called "Wonderful Hair Grower".

Role model

Breedlove saw her prosperity as a way of ***creating opportunities for others***, and she donated thousands to **African-American causes**. An accomplished speaker, her story of personal triumph **INSPIRED OTHER WOMEN** to "rise above laundry" and start their own businesses.

How she changed the world

Overcoming a tough start in life to work her way to the top, Breedlove used her wealth and fame to help fellow African-Americans. Her company is still in business today.

Who came after...

African-American **ANN FUDGE** *became the leader of the massive advertising agency Young & Rubicam in 2003, and was an adviser to US President Barack Obama.*

African-American **JANICE BRYANT HOWROYD** *launched Act-1 Group in 1978. Today, it is one of the largest employment agencies in the USA.*

Coco Chanel

The fashion TRAILBLAZER who gave the world the "little black dress"

Fashion pioneer

After her mother's early death, Coco Chanel was raised in an orphanage where **nuns taught her to sew**. In 1910, she opened her **FIRST BOUTIQUE** in Paris, France, and her innovative use of comfortable jersey fabric proved a big hit. By the 1920s, her business had expanded to include a fashion house, her own textile factory, and a line of perfumes. She went on to introduce the **legendary fragrance Chanel No. 5** and the "little black dress" to the fashion world.

> **By the way...**
> My real name is Gabrielle. "Coco" was my nickname when I sang in cabaret clubs as a young woman.

Chanel fashion house in Paris, France, in 1936

Decline and comeback

Chanel suffered **BAD PRESS** after having a relationship with a German Nazi officer during **World War II**. Returning to favour in the 1950s, she continued to design clothes until her death in 1971. Today, the Chanel label remains **one of the world's best-known luxury brands**.

How she changed...
Chanel's chic and comfortable designs revolutionized fashion. Her signature black dress is still popular today.

the world

Indian Institute of Management, in Kolkata, India, where Nooyi did her masters degree

Indra Nooyi

From India to the top of CORPORATE USA

Breaking the mould

Born in India, Nooyi was *raised in a conservative society* with rigid gender roles. After gaining degrees in chemistry and business administration, she worked as a **PRODUCT MANAGER**. She moved to the USA in 1978 to study at the **Yale School of Management**.

By the way...
As a young woman, I played a lot of a cricket and fronted an all-female rock band.

Influential innovator

Nooyi joined PepsiCo in 1994, and became **head of the company** in 2006. Under her management, the company has expanded, while making Pepsi's products **HEALTHIER**. She is regarded as one of the most *powerful women in business* today.

How she changed...
With hard work and determination, Nooyi became CEO of the world's second-largest drink and food business.

the world

Peggy Guggenheim
The PATRON of modern art

An eccentric socialite, American Peggy Guggenheim was instrumental in promoting modern art during the 20th century.

The Titanic

Family fortune

Born into fabulous wealth, Peggy Guggenheim was the niece of American art collector Solomon R. Guggenheim. Tragedy struck in 1912 when her father died in the sinking of the *Titanic*. **Coming into her inheritance** at the age of 21, Guggenheim **SET OFF TO SEE EUROPE**.

Wassily Kandinsky's Transverse Line

Did you know?
Guggenheim held a women-only exhibition in 1943, one of the first of its kind.

Free-spirited lifestyle

Finding sanctuary in **bohemian Paris, France**, Guggenheim fell in with its modernist artists and writers. In 1938, she **opened an art gallery in London, England**, that showcased artists including Frenchman Jean Cocteau and Russia's Wassily Kandinsky. Although it **CREATED A BUZZ IN THE ART WORLD**, the gallery lost money and Guggenheim returned to Paris.

Who came before...

American art collector **LOUISINE HAVEMEYER** developed a passion for the French artist Edgar Degas's work. She and her husband became the greatest collectors of Impressionist paintings.

Welsh sisters Gwendoline and Margaret Davies amassed one of Britain's largest art collections in the early 20th century. It is housed in the **NATIONAL MUSEUM OF WALES** in Cardiff.

Passionate art collector

With the onset of World War II, Guggenheim began **buying the works of artists** such as Spaniards Pablo Picasso and Joan Miró. As the Germans advanced into France, she fled to the USA. Her **SECOND GALLERY**, "Art of this Century", opened in New York in 1942, **exhibiting Cubist, surrealist, and abstract art**.

The Peggy Guggenheim Collection, a museum devoted to modern art, in Venice

By the way...
I once shaved off my eyebrows to shock my high-school classmates.

Return to Europe

After the war, Guggenheim **settled in Venice, Italy**, where she established herself in the Palazzo Venier dei Leoni. By the 1960s, she had **stopped collecting art**. After her death in 1979, her home was **OPENED TO THE PUBLIC** as a modern art museum. It attracts 400,000 visitors each year.

How she changed the world

Peggy Guggenheim's love of art was crucial to its development. Her support helped artists reach wider audiences. She was, in her own words, determined to "serve the future instead of recording the past".

Who came after...

American **AGNES GUND** has built up a personal collection to rival any museum. She is now the President Emerita of New York's Museum of Modern Art (MoMA).

Qatari art curator **SHEIKHA MAYASSA** is one of the most powerful people in the art world. In 2012, she oversaw the record-setting purchase of French artist Paul Cézanne's The Card Players for $250 million.

Oprah Winfrey

The SUPERSTAR of all media

Known for her hugely popular television talk show, African-American Oprah Winfrey is also an actor, publisher, producer, and philanthropist. Her rags-to-riches life story has inspired millions.

Winfrey winning an award in Nashville in 1971

Poor childhood

Born in Mississippi, USA, Winfrey's early years **were marred by poverty and neglect** – she was so poor as a child that she wore dresses made from potato sacks. Things began to improve when Winfrey went to **live with her father** in Nashville, Tennessee. Under his guidance, she **EXCELLED** at school and won a university scholarship.

Ratings revolution

Aged 19, Winfrey began *co-anchoring the local television news*, and by the age of 24, was **hosting a television chat show**. She joined talk show *A.M. Chicago* in 1984, which became the **WILDLY SUCCESSFUL** *Oprah Winfrey Show*. Winfrey's interviewing style and warm personality helped her to overcome the unspoken race and gender barriers in television and she soon dominated the ratings.

Did you know?
Winfrey holds such sway over public opinion that her influence has even been called "The Oprah Effect".

Who came before...

In the early 20th century, French director **ALICE GUY-BLACHÉ** became the first woman to found her own film studio. During her career, she oversaw the production of nearly 750 films.

American journalist and star of the Today programme **BARBARA WALTERS** paved the way for Winfrey and other female television personalities in the 20th century.

Billions in business

Winfrey set up **production company Harpo, Inc.** in 1986 and took ownership of her talk show. Her **MANY SUCCESSFUL VENTURES** include a book club and magazine. In 2011, she launched her *own cable TV channel*.

By the way...
My real name is "Orpah", from the Bible – but because no one could spell or pronounce it, I became Oprah.

Presidential Medal of Freedom

Charity work

Winfrey has **donated millions to charitable causes** – from education schemes in South Africa to **reconstruction in New Orleans**, USA, following Hurricane Katrina. In 2013, President Barack Obama awarded her the Presidential Medal of Freedom, the **HIGHEST CIVILIAN AWARD** in the USA.

How she changed the world

Winfrey overcame poverty and hardship to become the most influential woman in television, a media mogul, and the first African-American billionaire. Her story has shown that it is your attitude that determines your path in life.

What came after...

Winfrey's public support of presidential candidate **BARACK OBAMA** *in the 2008 Democratic primary race was estimated to have generated more than one million votes for Obama.*

American actor and comedian **ELLEN DEGENERES** *became a star on daytime TV with her talk show* The Ellen DeGeneres Show.

Internet impact
The TECH WOMEN
making digital waves

The Internet has opened up many new opportunities, and these women are shaking up the digital landscape.

Carol Bartz

American business executive Carol Bartz built her reputation at the *software developer* Autodesk. In 2009, she **TOOK CHARGE** of the struggling Internet giant Yahoo, becoming the **first female chief executive officer (CEO) of a major software company**.

Radia Perlman

In the 1970s and 1980s, scientists were busy working on the technology that would one day **lead to the Internet**. American software designer Radia Perlman's **INNOVATION** in 1985 of the "spanning tree protocol" allowed *larger numbers of interconnected computers* to communicate with one another more effectively.

By the way...
Perlman's vital contribution to the underlying structure of the Internet earned her the title "Mother of the Internet".

Sheryl Sandberg

Having cut her teeth at Google, American businesswoman Sheryl Sandberg joined the **world's largest social networking site**, Facebook, in 2008 as its chief operating officer. Her main achievement has been to make Facebook a *very profitable company*. She is also the first woman to sit on Facebook's **BOARD OF DIRECTORS**.

Martha Lane Fox

In the late 1990s, British businesswoman and philanthropist Martha Lane Fox found fame as the **co-founder of Europe's largest travel website**, Lastminute.com. Still making an impact, she inspired Dot Everyone – a public institution that aims to make digital technology **ACCESSIBLE** to all and *close the gender gap in the technology sector*.

Juliana Rotich

Kenyan-born Rotich is best known as one of the founders of the website **USHAHIDI**, which presents crisis areas around the world as **live, online maps** to raise awareness. She currently *campaigns for Internet access* for the world's estimated 4 billion plus people who are "offline".

achievers

1

3

The greatest success stories are from people who have buckets of self-belief and well-defined goals. Some are sporting legends at the top of their game, going for gold on the international stage; some are fearless aviators who take to the skies for record-breaking flights; while others are intrepid explorers, scaling mountains and mapping lands. All push themselves to the limit, and achieve things that once seemed impossible.

Althea Gibson

Grand Slam SUPERSTAR

Althea Gibson was the first African-American athlete to have a successful career as an international tennis player.

By the way... In my career I won 11 Grand Slam tournaments, including six doubles titles.

Men line up outside an unemployment office in Harlem, New York, in 1931.

From troubles to tennis

The terrible drought of the 1930s in South Carolina, USA, forced Althea Gibson's family to **leave their farm and move to New York City**. They lived in a *poor, African-American neighbourhood* called Harlem, where few people had jobs. Gibson **LEARNED TO PLAY TENNIS** at a community sports project for disadvantaged kids.

Who came before...

In 1948, **REGINALD WEIR** *became the first African-American to play a USLTA (United States Lawn Tennis Association) national championship.*

Four-time Olympic gold medallist **JESSE OWENS** *inspired African-American athletes. He was the first to be honoured with a ticker-tape parade in 1936. Gibson was the second.*

Tennis highs

Gibson had skill and she was prepared to work hard. She **IGNORED** people who thought tennis was only for white people. In 1951, she was the **first African-American player at the Wimbledon Championships in London, UK**. In 1957, she won Wimbledon and shook hands with Queen Elizabeth II, who presented her with the trophy. Soon, Gibson was *ranked number one* in the world.

In 1972, Gibson began heading a programme to bring tennis equipment to underprivileged city neighbourhoods.

Did you know?
Gibson was the first African-American woman to appear on the covers of Sports Illustrated and Time.

Wimbledon trophy

Golfing and later life

Gibson left the tennis world in around 1960, *disillusioned by racism in the sport*. She reinvented herself as a **professional golfer**, but still faced a lot of discrimination. Later, Gibson switched to something more worthy. She ran **OUTREACH PROGRAMMES** to bring sport to disadvantaged children.

How she changed the world

The first African-American woman to make it to the International Women's Sports Hall of Fame, Gibson also helped make tennis more diverse. Today, about a third of American tennis players are non-white.

Who came after...

Aboriginal Australian tennis player **EVONNE GOOLAGONG CAWLEY** *became a role model by winning 12 Grand Slam titles from 1971 to 1980.*

African-American tennis player **VENUS WILLIAMS** *has won 21 Grand Slam events and – along with her sister Serena – more Olympic golds than any other player.*

Nellie Bly

Around the WORLD in 72 days

Fearless American journalist Nellie Bly became a global celebrity when she took on a challenge to travel round the world in under 80 days – and succeeded.

Starting out

Nellie Bly got her **break** when she was only 18 years old. The *Pittsburgh Dispatch* newspaper published an article calling working women "a monstrosity". Bly wrote a **LETTER OF PROTEST** to the editor, who was so impressed that he hired her!

The Pittsburgh Dispatch building

The Blackwell's Island asylum in New York, USA, where Bly posed as a patient

Ace investigator

Bly made her name as **one of the world's first undercover reporters**, exposing scandals such as government corruption and **dangerous working conditions in factories**. She even pretended to be mentally ill so that she could **INVESTIGATE CRUEL TREATMENT** of patients at a hospital for the mentally ill.

UK

Japan

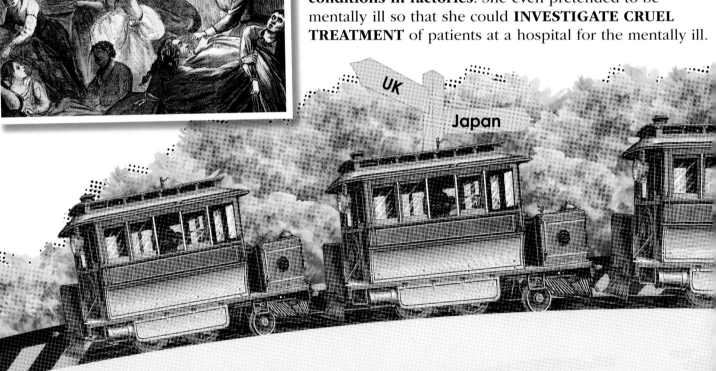

Who came before...

The first successful voyage to circumnavigate the Earth was embarked on in 1519. Portuguese sailor **FERDINAND MAGELLAN** led the expedition, which lasted three years, but Magellan himself was killed on the way.

In 1766, French woman **JEANNE BARÉ** became the first woman to sail round the world. She set off disguised as a male sailor.

Bly the globetrotter

In 1889, Bly set out from New Jersey, USA, on her **MOST DARING ASSIGNMENT** yet – to beat the "record" of Phineas Fogg, the fictional hero of the novel *Around the World in 80 Days* by French writer Jules Verne. She eventually **completed the trip** in 72 days, 6 hours, 11 minutes, and 14 seconds.

Did you know?
Bly was also an inventor – she designed a kind of milk can and a stackable rubbish bin.

The route taken by Bly on her world trip

By the way
My round-the-globe route included the USA, UK, France, Egypt, Singapore, Hong Kong, and Japan.

Eiffel Tower, Paris, France

How she changed the world
Nellie Bly was a real pioneer in journalism – as a woman, and because she created a new kind of undercover journalism. Her daredevil stunts and worldwide fame inspired other women to pursue their own adventurous ambitions.

Who came after...

American aviator **WILEY POST** *became the first pilot to fly solo round the world, in 1933. His flight took just under eight days.*

In 2012, Dutch sailor **LAURA DEKKER** *became the youngest person, at 16, to sail solo round the world.*

High fliers
INTREPID WOMEN who embarked on historic flights

The first people to fly aeroplanes or travel in space were men – but these courageous women were close on their tails.

Quimby crossed the English Channel in a Blériot XI monoplane.

Harriet Quimby

American journalist and screenwriter Harriet Quimby **TOOK UP FLYING AS A HOBBY** – but it is what she is most remembered for. She was the *first woman to gain a pilot's licence in the USA*, in 1911, and she became the **first woman to fly across the English Channel** the following year. Quimby died in an airshow accident aged just 37.

Did you know?
Shakhovskaya was a Russian princess. Tsar Nicholas II was her cousin.

Shakhovskaya flew one of the Wright Brothers' biplanes.

Eugenie Mikhailovna Shakhovskaya

Shakhovskaya trained as a pilot in Germany and then returned to her native Russia to **work for the Wright Brothers' aircraft company**. She became the *first female military pilot* when she flew **RECONNAISSANCE MISSIONS** in World War I, and may have been a spy. She was sentenced to death by firing squad for attempting to desert the army during the war, but she was eventually freed during the Russian Revolution of 1917.

Amelia Earhart

American aviator Amelia Earhart saw her first plane when she was 10 years old – and fell in love. She grew up to be the ***first woman to fly across the Atlantic*** and to co-found the 99s, an **international organization for female pilots**. Earhart went missing over the Pacific during an attempt to **FLY AROUND THE WORLD** in 1937.

Earhart's record-breaking solo transatlantic flight was made in a red Lockheed Vega 5B.

Johnson flew to Australia in a Gipsy Moth plane nicknamed "Jason".

Amy Johnson

Pioneering English pilot Amy Johnson made her name by **flying solo from England to Australia** in 1930. She was the first woman to make the 18,000-km (11,000-mile) flight. Johnson ***set more flying records in the 1930s***. She died in a **PLANE CRASH** in World War II: some say she was shot down by friendly fire (accidental weapon fire from one's own side).

Tereshkova orbited Earth 48 times in a Vostok 6 spacecraft.

Valentina Tereshkova

Soviet factory worker and amateur skydiver Valentina Tereshkova beat more than 400 other candidates to be the **FIRST WOMAN IN SPACE**, in 1963. She was **inducted into the Soviet Air Force** in order to join the space programme. During her three-day mission, she took some of the ***first photos of Earth's atmosphere from space***.

Gertrude Bell

EXPLORER of the desert

Best known for helping establish modern Iraq, Gertrude Bell was also a writer, archaeologist, spy, explorer, and mountaineer.

Brilliant student

Born into a **wealthy family** in Durham, UK, in 1868, Gertrude Bell always had a sense of adventure. Aged 17, she began **studying at Oxford University**, where she became the first woman to gain a **FIRST-CLASS DEGREE** in modern history.

Travels around the world

A trip Bell made to Tehran, Iran, in 1892, sparked a lifelong interest in the **Middle East and in Arabian culture**. Over the next decade, she developed a **passion for travelling and archaeology**. She wrote and published on the things she saw. Going deep into the Syrian and Arabian deserts, she **DOCUMENTED THE LANDS AND THEIR TRIBES**.

Did you know?
Bell spoke eight languages, and was fluent in Arabic, Persian, French, and German.

Who came before...

In 1813, eccentric British socialite and adventurer **LADY HESTER STANHOPE** became the first woman to cross the Syrian desert – but she had to disguise herself as a man to do it!

In the 19th century, British writer **ISABELLA BIRD**, called the "boldest of travellers", was the first female to become a Fellow of the prestigious Royal Geographical Society.

Creation of modern Iraq

After the outbreak of World War I in 1914, **British Intelligence recruited Bell** as an officer to help forge **ARAB ALLIANCES** against the Ottoman Empire. With the help of her maps and local knowledge, the British captured the enemy's southern capital of Baghdad. Bell helped to *define the boundaries of the new country of Iraq*, with Baghdad as its capital, and helped to choose its first ruler.

By the way...
In 1902, I spent 48 hours clinging to a rope while attempting to climb the Finsteraarhorn – the highest peak in the Swiss Alps.

Bell travelled to the city of Najaf (in modern-day Iraq) in 1911, and saw the Main Gate of the city.

Bell worked with British diplomat and archaeologist T. E. Lawrence during World War I.

Museum treasures

In the final years of her life, Bell's love of archaeology inspired her to *establish a museum*, now known as the **IRAQI NATIONAL MUSEUM**. She died soon after the museum's opening in 1926. She was posthumously **honoured** with the Order of the British Empire.

The Dome of the Rock is a shrine in the Old City of Jerusalem, which Bell visited for the first time in 1899.

How she changed the world

Bell was one of the most powerful women in the British Empire in the early 20th century. She achieved many "firsts", from climbing mountain peaks and exploring uncharted deserts, to being the first female intelligence officer in the British military.

Who came after...

British author **FREYA STARK** wrote books on her Middle East travels, and encouraged Arab support for the Allies during World War II.

The Iraq of Gertrude Bell lasted until 1958. Ten years later, the Arab Socialist Ba'ath party seized power. Ba'ath party leaders **AHMAD HASSAN AL-BAKR** and Saddam Hussein went on to govern the country.

Junko Tabei

FEARLESS Japanese mountaineer

Pioneering female climber Junko Tabei was the first woman to scale Mount Everest, the world's highest mountain.

Tabei became passionate about mountaineering after climbing Mount Nasu, Japan, when she was 10 years old.

Seeking the high life

As a student, Junko Tabei **began mountaineering**. After she graduated, she founded the **LADIES' CLIMBING CLUB (LCC)** in Japan. At that time, women in Japan did not enjoy the same freedoms as men, and were expected to stay at home and raise children. *Tabei had different plans*.

Who came before...

Mount Everest is named after Welsh surveyor and geographer **GEORGE EVEREST**. The mountain is also called Sagarmatha in Nepal, and Chomolungma in Tibet.

In 1953, New Zealand's **EDMUND HILLARY** and his Nepalese guide **TENZING NORGAY** were the first people to scale Everest.

Conquering Everest

In 1975, 35-year-old Tabei set out to climb Mount Everest – 8,848 m (29,029 ft) above sea level – with the LCC. Disaster struck nearly three-quarters of the way up when *an avalanche engulfed their camp*. Knocked **UNCONSCIOUS**, Tabei had to be dug out of the snow by the expedition's Sherpas (skilled mountaineers who live near the Himalayan mountain range). Just 12 days after the avalanche that nearly killed her, Tabei became the **first female to reach the top** of Mount Everest.

Map showing the Seven Summits

Denali

Elbrus

Everest

Kilimanjaro

Aconcagua

Puncak Jaya

Vinson Massif

By the way...
Our 1975 expedition had little funding, so we had to make our own equipment and sleeping bags to save money.

Keep on climbing

After Everest, Tabei *went on to climb the remaining six of the Seven Summits*. She campaigns for climbers and tourists to conserve mountain environments, and her current goal is to scale the **HIGHEST MOUNTAIN** in every country. She's **climbed more than 60** of them so far.

How she changed the world

Faced with some of the toughest challenges on Earth, Tabei's determination to succeed has seen her achieve her dreams, and inspire countless others.

Who came after...

In 2010, Spanish mountaineer **EDURNE PASABAN** *became the first woman to climb the 14 eight-thousanders – mountains with peaks over 8,000 m (26,247 ft) above sea level.*

The first woman to climb the eight-thousanders without oxygen tanks was Austrian mountaineer **GERLINDE KALTENBRUNNER**, *in 2011.*

Wilma Rudolph

The bedridden child who battled illness to become the world's FASTEST woman

Slow start

Born **prematurely** into a large African-American family in 1940, Wilma Rudolph suffered from polio as a child. By the age of nine, she was strong enough to play basketball, and she *tried track races at school*. After winning a place on the US Olympics team, she took home a **BRONZE MEDAL** for the 400 m relay in the 1956 Olympics.

Did you know?
Rudolph entered the Black Sports Hall of Fame in 1973, and the National Track and Field Hall of Fame in 1974.

How she changed...
Rudolph was the first American woman to win three gold medals at an Olympic Games, making her a role model for female athletes.
the world

Rudolph holds the gold medals she won at the 1960 Olympics in Rome.

Fast track

At the 1960 Olympics, **Rudolph won the 100 m and 200 m races, and the 400 m relay**. The champion returned to her hometown of Clarksville, Tennessee, USA, for a **VICTORY PARADE**. At Rudolph's request, both *blacks and whites were allowed to celebrate together*. It was the first integrated event in the city's history.

Nova Peris

The Aboriginal Australian who INSPIRED her people to celebrate their identity

There are more than 600,000 Australian Aboriginal people.

Gold run

Nova Peris was a sporty Aboriginal (native Australian) teenager from Darwin, Australia, who joined the national women's hockey team. When they won at the 1996 Olympics, Peris became the **first Aboriginal Australian to win gold**. She also **EXCELLED AT RUNNING**, winning in two events at the Commonwealth Games in 1998. This made her the *first Australian to win gold in two sports*.

Political pioneer

When Peris **RETIRED**, she started painting Aboriginal art and designing commemorative Olympic coins. Peris also *set up a charity to promote a healthy lifestyle* for Aboriginal children. In 2013, she became the **first Aboriginal woman elected to Australia's federal parliament**.

How she changed...

After going for gold in two sporting fields, Peris has worked tirelessly to improve the lives of Australia's Aboriginal population.

the world

Serena Williams
Grand Slam CHAMP

The best female player in the history of the game, this tennis titan is one of the 21st century's most celebrated sports people.

The Williams sisters, Venus and Serena (on the right), with their father

Toddler tennis
Serena Jameka Williams was born in Michigan, USA, in 1981. She and her **older sister, Venus**, were introduced to tennis by their *enthusiastic father* at an early age – Serena was just three at the time! In California's junior circuit, both sisters managed to receive **NUMBER-ONE RANKINGS**.

Taking titles
After joining the Rick Macci Tennis Academy in Florida, USA, Serena **turned professional** in 1995. In 1999, the Williams sisters became **CHAMPIONS** of Wimbledon and the US Open in the ladies' doubles. Serena was also *victorious* in the singles competition in the US Open that year, becoming the second African-American woman to win the tournament.

Did you know?
The phrase "Serena Slam" describes Serena's feat of winning all four Grand Slam singles titles in 2002–2003.

Who came before...

In 1567, MARY, QUEEN OF SCOTS, became the first woman to play the game of golf in Scotland.

British skater MADGE SYERS competed alongside men at the 1902 World Figure Skating Championships and took silver, leading to the creation of a separate women's competition.

Number one

Serena became the **NUMBER ONE** player in 2002 when she won the US Open, French Open, Wimbledon, and the Australian Open (in early 2003). She continues to *rack up titles*, winning a seventh Wimbledon title in 2016, taking her **total tally of Grand Slam singles wins to 22**. She is now just three titles away from breaking the record, currently held by Australian Margaret Court.

The speed of Serena's fastest serve

207	KM/H
128.6	MPH

By the way...
I have won four Olympic gold medals across three Olympic games, three of them in doubles with Venus.

Perhaps the greatest ever female tennis player, Serena has dominated the game since the late 1990s. Her powerhouse performances inspire fans and athletes across the world.

How she changed the world

Czech-American **MARTINA NAVRATILOVA** won 18 Grand Slam titles, including a record-breaking nine Wimbledon wins.

Winner of 22 major tennis titles, German tennis player **STEFFI GRAF** made history with her Golden Grand Slam (the big four plus Olympic gold) in 1988.

Tanni Grey-Thompson

The Welsh WHEELCHAIR RACER who became a baroness in the House of Lords

Paralympian prowess

Born with spina bifida, a condition that left her legs paralysed, Tanni Grey-Thompson began wheelchair racing at 13. **Representing Great Britain, she won a total of 16 medals** over five Paralympic Games, competing in the 100 m, 200 m, 400 m, and 800 m, and in the 400 m relay. She also won the women's wheelchair race of the **LONDON MARATHON** six times between 1992 and 2002.

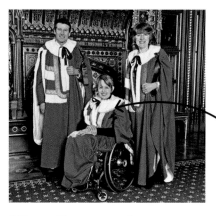

Grey-Thompson is inducted into the House of Lords as a baroness.

Life after sport

Since **retiring from sport in 2007**, Grey-Thompson has dedicated her time to *sport and disability issues*. She often gives her expert opinion on sport for TV and radio shows. In 2010, she was rewarded for all her achievements with a seat in the **HOUSE OF LORDS** (the upper house of the UK parliament), where she uses her experience and knowledge to contribute to debates.

How she changed...

As a famous and successful athlete, Grey-Thompson has inspired countless people and helped make sport more accessible.

the world

Jessica Ennis-Hill

Olympic HEPTATHLON CHAMPION and winner of three World Championship golds

Versatile sportswoman

Track and field athletes who are brilliant all-rounders can show off their skills by *specializing in multi-events*, such as the heptathlon, which consists of seven events: 100 m hurdles, high jump, shot put, 200 m, 800 m, long jump, and javelin. British athlete Jessica Ennis-Hill was just 20 when she announced her arrival on the senior international stage by winning a **COMMONWEALTH GAMES BRONZE** for the heptathlon.

High jump

Shot put

Hurdles

By the way...
I've held the British records for the 100 m hurdles, high jump, and indoor pentathlon (which consists of five events).

International career

In the **2012 Olympics in London, UK**, Ennis-Hill racked up a **BRITISH RECORD SCORE** as she took the heptathlon gold in front of her home fans. *More accolades followed*, including a gold at the 2015 World Championships in Beijing, China, and a silver in the 2016 Olympics in Rio de Janeiro, Brazil.

How she changed...
By competing at the highest level in one of the toughest sports, Ennis-Hill has shown herself to be one of the most impressive athletes in her field.

the world

2

1

3

Marta

Football's FINEST female forward

The brilliance of Brazilian Marta has bagged her World Player of the Year a record-breaking five times.

By the way...
My feet have been immortalized in concrete at Brazil's celebrated Estádio do Maracanã (Maracanã Stadium).

Young people playing football in the streets of Rio de Janeiro.

On the ball

Born in 1986, *Marta Vieira da Silva* grew up surrounded by street football. She was **talent-spotted playing on a boys' team** and moved to Vasco da Gama in Rio de Janeiro, Brazil. She spent two years there, honing her skills for the women's club, before moving on to another Brazilian club, Santa Cruz. In 2004, she left Brazil to play in **SWEDEN** for Umeå IK.

Did you know?
Marta is nicknamed "Pelé con faldas" (Pelé with skirts) after Pelé, the famous Brazilian footballer.

What came before...

In 1895, one of the FIRST OFFICIAL WOMEN'S FOOTBALL MATCHES *took place, with North London beating South London 7-1.*

The first international women's game was held in 1920. **DICK KERR'S LADIES** *from Preston, UK, beat a French side 2-0 in Paris, France, watched by 25,000 fans.*

Sublime skills

Marta became a **footballing giant** in both the midfield and striker positions. She won six Swedish leagues with Umeå IK and two more in the USA for Los Angeles Sol. From 2006, she was named *FIFA World Player of the Year* five consecutive times. She has scored 15 goals for Brazil in four World Cups, a **RECORD** for the competition.

Global ambassador

Marta has gained recognition as an international sporting star and spokesperson. She was made **Goodwill Ambassador for the United Nations** in 2010, *standing up for women's rights and people from less privileged backgrounds*. She became an **AMBASSADOR FOR THE MEN'S WORLD CUP** in Brazil in 2014, alongside five legends from the men's game.

Marta meets the women's football team from Sierra Leone, Africa.

Marta is fluent in Portuguese, English, and Swedish.

How she changed the world

In a sport dominated by men, Marta has shone the spotlight on women's football. Relying only on her skills and determination, she has risen to the top to be the best female footballer of all time. She leads the global drive to bring more players and fans to the beautiful game.

What came after...

During the 1970s, the FIRST PART-TIME PROFESSIONAL WOMEN'S LEAGUE *was established in Italy. Other countries followed suit and set up leagues of their own.*

In 1991, the first **FIFA WOMEN'S WORLD CUP** *tournament was held, with the USA taking the trophy. The first women's football tournament at the Olympics was staged five years later.*

Let's applaud...

These extraordinary women made their mark on the history of BRITAIN and IRELAND.

Boudicca (c.30–c.60)

In 60 CE, this *fiery warrior queen* of the Celtic Iceni people **LED A MAJOR UPRISING** against the **occupying Roman forces**, and tried – but failed – to kick them out of Britain.

The name Boudicca was derived from the Celtic word for "victory".

Aethelflaed (c.870–918)

Anglo-Saxon princess Aethelflaed was the eldest daughter of Alfred the Great, wife of Aethelred of Mercia (a kingdom of central England), and Mercia's ruler from 911. She **BUILT UP** her *country's defences* against invading Vikings.

Grace O'Malley (c.1530–c.1603)

Born into a powerful Irish **seafaring family**, clan chief and pirate O'Malley *raided ships* off the west coast of Ireland. She supported rebels **AGAINST ENGLISH RULE** and met with Elizabeth I in 1593.

Mary, Queen of Scots (1542–1587)

Mary **became queen at six days old**. In 1567, she had to *give up the throne* to her baby son, James VI, and flee to England. Elizabeth I of England saw Mary as a **THREAT**, and imprisoned and later beheaded her.

Margaret Hughes (c.1630–1719)

Hughes was the *first professional female actor on the English stage*. Theatre was **FLOURISHING**, and Hughes **appeared in plays** by great dramatists such as John Dryden.

Aphra Behn (c.1640–1689)

Behn grew up when England was ruled by Oliver Cromwell, after the execution of King Charles I, and was a **SUPPORTER** of the king's exiled son, **Charles II**. Although she made her name as a *playwright, poet, and translator*, she may have also worked as a spy.

Mary Somerville (1780–1872)

Scottish mathematician and astronomer Somerville *predicted the existence of Neptune*. She and German astronomer **Caroline Herschel** were the **FIRST FEMALE MEMBERS** of the Royal Astronomical Society.

Elizabeth Fry (1780–1845)

Nicknamed the "angel of prisons", English social reformer Fry *worked to improve conditions* for prisoners. She also set up a **school for nurses and a night shelter** for the **HOMELESS**.

Grace Darling (1815–1842)

In 1838, Darling and her father *braved rough seas* off northeast England to **RESCUE** survivors of the sinking paddlesteamer *Forfarshire* in their rowing boat. The steamer had **run aground off the coast**.

Octavia Hill (1838–1912)

Eager to *improve life for the poor*, English social reformer Hill worked to create **SOCIAL HOUSING** (accommodation provided by the state or charities) and public parks. She was also one of the **founders of the National Trust**.

The Edinburgh Seven

In 1869, this group of **seven women** were the first to study **MEDICINE**, at Edinburgh University despite *hostile opposition*.

Lady Augusta Gregory (1852–1932)

Lady Gregory helped to **CREATE A REVIVAL** in Irish literature that *celebrated folklore and myths*. She **co-founded** Ireland's national theatre, the Abbey Theatre, in Dublin.

Hertha Ayrton (1854–1923)

In 1899, British engineer Ayrton *explained the science* of why street lamps hissed. She later invented the **AYRTON FAN**, which helped blow away poison gas in the **World War I** trenches.

Elsie Inglis (1864–1917)

Doctor and suffragette Inglis **founded the Scottish Women's Hospitals for Foreign Service** in 1914. It sent medical staff abroad *to set up hospitals* to aid the **WAR EFFORT**.

Countess Constance Markievicz (1868–1927)

Countess Markievicz fought for **IRISH INDEPENDENCE**. In 1918, she was the **first female to be elected to the British parliament**, but *she refused to take her seat* in protest at British rule. She was imprisoned many times.

Hanna Sheehy-Skeffington (1877–1946)

Ireland's most celebrated **SUFFRAGETTE** set up the *Irish Womens' Workers Union* and a newspaper to champion women's rights. In 1918, some Irish women were granted the **right to vote**.

Megan Lloyd George (1902–1966)

Lloyd George followed her prime minister father David into **POLITICS** – in 1929, she was the *first female member of parliament (MP) for a Welsh constituency*. She rose to Deputy Leader of the Liberals but later joined the **Labour party**.

Jocelyn Bell (born 1943)

In the late 1960s, Northern Irish Bell *identified* the first **PULSARS** (spinning neutron stars that emit radio waves). Controversially, the discovery won Bell's supervisor, not Bell, the **Nobel Prize**.

Kate Adie (born 1945)

Pioneering English journalist Adie has **REPORTED** from **dangerous war zones** around the world. She came to prominence when she bravely covered the *siege of the Iranian Embassy* in London, UK, in 1980.

Zaha Hadid (1950–2016)

Iraqi-born British architect Hadid **DESIGNED** the Guangzhou Opera House in China and the London Aquatic Centre for the 2012 Olympics. She was the **first female to win** the *Pritzker Architecture Prize*.

Theresa May (born 1956)

May became a **CONSERVATIVE PARTY** MP in 1997, after a **career in banking**. In June 2016, she became the *UK's second female prime minister*.

Helen Sharman (born 1963)

The **first Briton in space**, Sharman responded to a radio advertisement to be an **ASTRONAUT**. She launched into space in 1991, and *spent eight days on the Mir space station*.

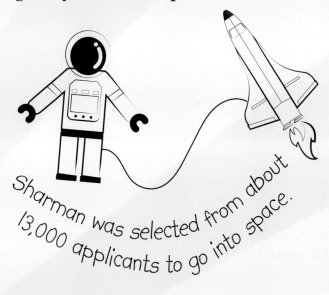

Sharman was selected from about 13,000 applicants to go into space.

Nicola Sturgeon (born 1970)

Sturgeon was elected to the **Scottish Parliament** in 1999. In 2014, she became both the *first female leader* of the Scottish National Party and the first female **FIRST MINISTER** of Scotland.

Zadie Smith (born 1975)

Jamaican-English writer Smith *landed onto the literary scene* in 2000 with her novel *White Teeth*. It explored **themes** such as race and immigration, and won many **INTERNATIONAL PRIZES**.

Glossary

Atom
The smallest particle of a chemical element that has the properties of that element.

Boycott
An action in which people stop commercial or social relations as an act of punishment or protest.

Civil Rights Movement
A campaign that started in the USA during the 1960s with the aim of giving people the same rights regardless of their skin colour.

Communism
A system of government in which a country's people hold property in common and each person contributes to society according to his or her ability and needs.

Concentration camp
A type of jail in which political prisoners, prisoners of war, or persecuted minorities are kept and do hard labour or await execution.

Corruption
Any type of dishonest, immoral, or illegal action, often on the part of a country's ruling leader or government.

Democracy
A society in which the people have a say in how their government is run.

Dictatorship
A society in which the government is ruled completely by an individual or small group. The leader, or dictator, has absolute power.

Double-helix structure
The spiral, ladder-shaped structure of deoxyribonucleic acid (DNA) – the genetic code for almost all forms of life.

Electron
A subatomic particle with a negative charge that orbits an atom's nucleus.

Evolution
The scientific theory that all living things have developed gradually over long periods of time.

Feminism
A cause aiming to give women the same rights and opportunities as men.

Gene
A part of deoxyribonucleic acid (DNA) that determines a particular characteristic (such as eye colour) based on traits passed down generations.

Neutron
A subatomic particle with no charge, which is found in an atom's nucleus.

Nuclear energy
A type of energy released in one of two ways – by joining atoms together to make a larger atom (fusion) or by splitting an atom (fission).

Nucleus
The centre of an atom, which contains protons and neutrons.

Pacifism
The belief that problems can be resolved peacefully without war, conflict, or violence.

Paganism
A group of religions that often base their practices on the worship of traditional gods. Paganism precedes monotheistic religions like Christianity and Islam.

Proton
A subatomic particle with a positive charge, which is found in an atom's nucleus.

Racial segregation
The policy of separating racial groups.

Radioactivity
The emission of a powerful form of energy when atoms break down. Exposure to this intense energy is harmful to the human body.

Revolutionary
A person who fights for radical change in society by challenging accepted policies, sometimes through forceful or violent means.

Socialism
An economic system in which the workers control the production and distribution of goods themselves.

Suffragette Movement
A movement led by women to win the right to vote in political elections.

Taliban
An Islamic militant group that took over Afghanistan in 1995 and was overturned by US-led forces in 2001. It has since regrouped in the region.

Trade union
Employees in the same company or industry who unite as a group to negotiate with employers over contracts, benefits, and working conditions.

Tsar
A king or emperor of Russia before 1917.

USSR
The Union of Soviet Socialist Republics, which included most of the former Russian Empire. It existed from 1922 to 1991.

Index

Acknowledgements

DK WOULD LIKE TO THANK:
Jackie Brind for the index; Victoria Pyke for proofreading; Hansa Babra, Kshitiz Dobhal, Amisha Gupta, Neetika Malik Jhingan, and Arun Pottirayil for design assistance; and Anita Kakar for editorial assistance.

THE PUBLISHER WOULD LIKE TO THANK THE FOLLOWING FOR THEIR KIND PERMISSION TO REPRODUCE THEIR PHOTOGRAPHS:
(Key: a-above; b-below/bottom; c-centre; f-far; l-left; r-right; t-top)

1 Getty Images: Don Cravens (clb, cb). **3 123RF.com:** leftleg (clb/HAND). **Alamy Stock Photo:** Epa B.v. / Mk Chaudhry (clb); Friedrich Stark (clb/students); Epa B.v. / Bilawal (bl/Girls). **Getty Images:** Paul Ellis / AFP (bl). **8 123RF.com:** Georgios Kollidas (ca). **9 123RF.com:** Malgorzata Kistryn (r). **Getty Images:** IndiaPictures / Universal Images Group (c). **10 Alamy Stock Photo:** Lebrecht Music and Arts Photo Library (cl). **Fotolia:** Dario Sabljak (cl/Golden frame). **Getty Images:** PHAS / Universal Images Group (bl). **PENGUIN and the Penguin logo are trademarks of Penguin Books Ltd:** Wuthering Heights Emily Bronte, S.E. Hinton Puffin Classics (bc). **11 Alamy Stock Photo:** CSU Archives / Everett Collection (bc); Photo Researchers, Inc (cla); Granger, NYC. / Granger Historical Picture Archive (ca); Pictorial Press Ltd (bl). **12 Alamy Stock Photo:** Pictorial Press Ltd (cra). **Getty Images:** Frank Worth, Courtesy of Capital Art / Hulton Archive (bl). **13 Alamy Stock Photo:** A.F. Archive (tl, crb); Moviestore collection Ltd (bl). **14-15 Rex by Shutterstock:** Everett Collection (c). **14 Courtesy of the Maryland Historical Society:** White Studio / Eubie Blake Photograph Collection (cl). **Getty Images:** Michael Ochs Archives (br). **15 Alamy Stock Photo:** Ricky Fitchett / ZUMA Wire / ZUMA press (tc). **Getty Images:** MENAGER Georges / Paris Match Archive (tc). **Library of Congress, Washington, D.C.:** (cra). **Photoshot:** Pete Mariner / Retna (bl). **16 Alamy Stock Photo:** France Soir / Photos 12 (tl). **Dreamstime.com:** Laifa (cl). **Getty Images:** Keystone-France / Gamma-Keystone (br). **17 Alamy Stock Photo:** ZUMA Press Inc (b). **Dreamstime.com:** Olegslabinskiy (tr). **Getty Images:** Moore / Hulton Archive (ca). **18 Alamy Stock Photo:** Granger Historical Picture Archive (tr, cl). **Dorling Kindersley:** Durham University Oriental Museum (bl). **Getty Images:** Bettmann (cb). **Wellcome Images http://creativecommons.org/licenses/by/4.0/:** Iconographic Collections (bc). **19 Alamy Stock Photo:** The Artchives / Banco de México Diego Rivera Frida Kahlo Museums Trust, Mexico, D.F. / DACS / © DACS 2016 (tl); John Mitchell (cr); Scott Houston (tc). **Library of Congress, Washington, D.C.:** (bl). **20 Alamy Stock Photo:** The Art Archive (crb). **Getty Images:** JTB Photo / Universal Images Group (bl). **21 Bridgeman Images:** De Agostini Picture Library (tl); Granamour Weems Collection (bl). **Dreamstime.com:** Georgios Kollidas (r). **22 Alamy Stock Photo:** H. Armstrong Roberts / ClassicStock (cra); dpa picture alliance archive (cl). **Dreamstime.com:** Pictac (crb). **Getty Images:** Hulton Archive (bc); PHAS / Prisma / UIG (bl). **23 Alamy Stock Photo:** United Archives GmbH (ca). **PENGUIN and the Penguin logo are trademarks of Penguin Books Ltd:** The Diary of a Young Girl , Anne Frank (cb). **Press Association Images:** AP (bl). **24 Alamy Stock Photo:** Gregg Mancuso / Globe Photos / Zumapress.com (tc); sjvinyl / JoniMitchell.com (cl). **25 123RF.com:** Andrei Zaripov (cl/Book). **Alamy Stock Photo:** ZUMA Press, Inc (cra). **Dreamstime.com:** Luis Alvarenga / Liquoricelegs (cl). **Getty Images:** Jenny Anderson / Wireimage (tl). **28 Alamy Stock Photo:** Gianni Dagli Orti / The Art Archive (bc); Mary Evans Picture Library (cl). **Dorling Kindersley:** The Science Museum, London (tr). **Dreamstime.com:** Frenta (tl). **Wellcome Images http://creativecommons.org/licenses/by/4.0/:** Rare Books (bl). **29 Alamy Stock Photo:** epa european pressphoto agency b.v. (br); Mary Evans Picture Library (tr). **Getty Images:** 517398340 (tl). **Wellcome Images http://creativecommons.org/licenses/by/4.0/:** Iconographic Collections (bl). **30 akg-images:** Archives CDA / St-Genès (cla). **Alamy Stock Photo:** Pictorial Press Ltd (cr). **Getty Images:** Dea / G. Dagli Orti (bc). **31 Alamy Stock Photo:** Library of Congress / RGB Ventures / SuperStock (cl); The Print Collector (bl). **Dorling Kindersley:** The Science Museum (tl). **Getty Images:** Science & Society Picture Library (c). **32 Alamy Stock Photo:** The Natural History Museum (cr, bl); World History Archive (bc). **33 Alamy Stock Photo:** The Natural History Museum (tl). **Wellcome Images http://creativecommons.org/licenses/by/4.0/:** Archives & Manuscripts (cra); General Collections (bl). **34 Dreamstime.com:** Galina Ermolaeva (tr). **Getty Images:** Heritage Images / Hulton Archive (c). **35 Alamy Stock Photo:** Lebrecht Music and Arts Photo Library (tr); Photo Researchers, Inc (tl, c). **Dorling Kindersley:** Churchill College Archives, Cambridge University (clb). **Getty Images:** AFP (bl). **36 Alamy Stock Photo:** Granger Historical Picture Archive (bl). **Getty Images:** Culture Club (bl). **Wellcome Images http://creativecommons.org/licenses/by/4.0/:** Iconographic Collections (cla). **37 Alamy Stock Photo:** Akademie (tc); Granger Historical Picture Archive (bc). **Getty Images:** Apic / Hulton Archive (tl). **Science Photo Library:** Library of Congress (cra). **Wellcome Images http://creativecommons.org/licenses/by/4.0/:** (bl). **38 Dorling Kindersley:** Barrie Watts (bl). **Mary Evans Picture Library:** Winchester College / In aid of Mary Seacole

Memorial Statue Appeal (cl). **Wellcome Images http://creativecommons.org/licenses/by/4.0/:** Iconographic Collections (crb). **39 Derwen College:** (cr). **Library of Congress, Washington, D.C.:** (tl). **Averil Mansfield:** (bl). **40 Alamy Stock Photo:** Gabbro (cl); Photo Researchers, Inc (cra). **Getty Images:** Bettmann (bl); Library of Congress (bc). **41 Alamy Stock Photo:** Photo Researchers, Inc (tr). **Melissa Franklin:** Reidar Hahn / Fermi lab (bl). **Getty Images:** Pier Marco Tacca (bc). **42 123RF.com:** Maurizio Giovanni Bersanelli (cb/gorilla). **Alamy Stock Photo:** Arco Images GmbH / Vnoucek, F. (bl); Liam White (bc). **Getty Images:** Neil Selkirk / The LIFE Images Collection (c). **SuperStock:** Minden Pictures (cb/Mountain Gorilla). **43 123RF.com:** robert hyrons (clb); Naveen kalwa (cr). **Alamy Stock Photo:** epa european pressphoto agency b.v / Lucas Dolega (c). **44 Alamy Stock Photo:** World History Archive (cra). **Wellcome Images http://creativecommons.org/licenses/by/4.0/:** Iconographic Collections (bl); Science Museum, London / Medical Photographic Library (bc). **45 123RF.com:** broukoid (bl). **Getty Images:** Bettmann (c); De Agostini Picture Library (tr); Mario Tama (bc). **Science Photo Library:** King's College London Archives (cla). **48 Alamy Stock Photo:** Granger Historical Picture Archive (tr); Dorling Kindersley: Banbury Museum (bc). **Dreamstime.com:** Italianestro (cb). **Getty Images:** Heritage Images / Hulton Fine Art Collection (ca). **49 Alamy Stock Photo:** Granger Historical Picture Archive (tr, cb). **Library of Congress, Washington, D.C.:** (tl). **50 Alamy Stock Photo:** Mary Evans Picture Library (cl); North Wind Picture Archives (bl). **Getty Images:** Universal Images Group (ca). **Library of Congress, Washington, D.C.:** Popular Graphic Arts (bc). **50-51 Alamy Stock Photo:** North Wind Picture Archives (c). **51 Alamy Stock Photo:** Granger Historical Picture Archive (bc); Philip Scalia (cra). **52 Alamy Stock Photo:** The Art Archive (c); Interfoto (tl). **Getty Images:** adoc-photos (ca); Pierre Ogeron (bl). **53 Alamy Stock Photo:** Akademie (cb/Nobel Prize); Interfoto (c); akg-images (clb). **Dreamstime.com:** Italianestro (bl); Peter Probst (tl). **54 Getty Images:** ullstein bild (clb); Hulton Archive (cra). **55 Getty Images:** Chung Sung-Jun (bl); Alfred Eisenstaedt / The LIFE Picture Collection (cl); Gianluigi Guercia / AFP (cr). **56 Alamy Stock Photo:** Mary Evans Picture Library (bl); Keystone-France / Gamma-Keystone (tc). **56-57 Alamy Stock Photo:** Archive Pics (c/suffragettes). **Getty Images:** Heritage Images / Hulton Archive (c). **57 Alamy Stock Photo:** Hilary Morgan (cr). **Mary Evans Picture Library:** Peter Higginbotham Collection (tr). **58 Alamy Stock Photo:** age fotostock (c); Berliner Verlag / Berliner Verlag (br); Heritage Image Partnership Ltd (tl). **59 akg-images:** George (Jürgen) Wittenstein (c). **Alamy Stock Photo:** Pictorial Press Ltd (tl). **Dreamstime.com:** Italianestro (cb). **60-61 Getty Images:** Don Cravens (c). **60 Alamy Stock Photo:** Everett Collection Historical (cl); Granger Historical Picture Archive (ca); World History Archive (bc). **Press Association Images:** Julie Jacobson / AP (bc). **61 Dreamstime.com:** Palinchak (bc). **Getty Images:** Don Cravens (c); Steve Schapiro / Corbis Premium Historical (cr); Rolls Press / Popperfoto (bl). **62 Alamy Stock Photo:** ITAR-TASS News Agency (bc). **Dreamstime.com:** Simon Jeacle (cl). **Getty Images:** Ullstein bild (bl). **63 Getty Images:** Mark Reinstein / Corbis News (tl). **Reuters:** Corinne Dufka (cra). **Rex by Shutterstock:** Benjamin Lozovsky / BFA (bl); Benjamin Lozovsky / BFA (bc). **64-65 Alamy Stock Photo:** Epa B.v. / Mk Chaudhry (c); Friedrich Stark (c/Students); Epa B.v. / Bilawal (c/Girls). **Getty Images:** Paul Ellis / AFP (bc). **64 123RF.com:** leftleg (tc). **Alamy Stock Photo:** EPA B.v. / Maciej Kulczynski POLAND OUT (bc). **Getty Images:** Pete Marovich (bl). **65 Alamy Stock Photo:** Luiz Rampelotto / EuropaNewswire (bl); Gonçalo Silva (bc). **Getty Images:** AFP (tc, cr). **68 Alamy Stock Photo:** Classic Image (cra); Granger Historical Picture Archive (clb). **Getty Images:** Culture Club / Hulton Archive (bl); Hulton Archive (bc). **69 123RF.com:** Maria Itina (c). **Alamy Stock Photo:** Yolanda Perera Sánchez (bl). **Getty Images:** Kean Collection / Archive Photos (cra); Stock Montage (tl); Time Life Pictures (cl). **Library of Congress, Washington, D.C.:** Bain Collection (bc). **70 Getty Images:** Hulton Archive (bl). **71 Alamy Stock Photo:** Antiques & Collectables (tr); IanDagnall Computing (br). **72 Alamy Stock Photo:** Artokoloro Quint Lox Limited (cra); Sputnik (cl); Granger Historical Picture Archive (br); Chris Hellier (bc). **Dreamstime.com:** Italianestro (cb). **Getty Images:** Heritage Images / Hulton Fine Art Collection (cr). **72-73 Alamy Stock Photo:** The Print Collector (c). **73 Alamy Stock Photo:** Active Museum (c); Lanmas (bl). **Getty Images:** Heritage Images / Hulton Archive (tr). **Library of Congress, Washington, D.C.:** Popular Graphic Arts (bc). **74 123RF.com:** Sanchai Loongroong (cl). **Alamy Stock Photo:** Chronicle (crb). **Bridgeman Images:** Musee Guimet, Paris, France / Archives Charmet (cr). **75 Alamy Stock Photo:** Photo12 / Elk-Opid (cl); Mary Evans Picture Library (tr). **Bridgeman Images:** Royal Asiatic Society, London, UK (b). **76 Alamy Stock Photo:** Digital Image Library (cl); Heritage Image Partnership Ltd (cl); Falkensteinfoto (bc). **Dreamstime.com:** Italianestro (cr). **77 Alamy Stock Photo:** Falkensteinfoto (tr). **Dorling Kindersley:** National Maritime Museum, London (tl). **Getty Images:** Print Collector / Hulton Fine Art Collection (tl). **Photoshot:** (bc). **78 Alamy Stock Photo:** Granger Historical Picture Archive (cl). **Getty Images:** James L. Amos (bl). **78-79 Alamy Stock Photo:** Granger Historical

Archive (c). **79 123RF.com:** wrangel (tr). **Alamy Stock Photo:** nsf (bc). **Getty Images:** Archive Photos (bl). **80 Amura Yachts & Lifestyle:** www.amuraworld.com / en / topics / history-art-and-culture / articles / 272-maria-quiteria-de-jesus-the-heroine-of-brazil. **81 Alamy Stock Photo:** Interfoto (tl). **The Art Archive:** CCI (cr). **82-83 123RF.com:** Songquan Deng (c). **82 Alamy Stock Photo:** Josse Christophel (ac); Mary Evans Picture Library (cl); GL Archive (bl). **83 Alamy Stock Photo:** Everett Collection Historical (c, bl). **Getty Images:** Bettmann (cla, cra); Jeff J Mitchell (bc). **84 123RF.com:** Ivan Aleshin (bl). **Alamy Stock Photo:** Tetra Images (cr). **Bridgeman Images:** De Agostini Picture Library / A. Dagli Orti (cla). **Getty Images:** Dungan / The LIFE Images Collection (cb); Murali / The LIFE Images Collection (bc). **85 Getty Images:** The India Today Group (bl); Garofalo Jack (tl); Robert Nickelsberg / The LIFE Images Collection (tr). **86 123RF.com:** leftleg (c/Hand). **Alamy Stock Photo:** Slim Plantagenate (c). **Getty Images:** ullstein bild (tr); Keystone-France / Gamma-Keystone (bl). **87 123RF.com:** Enrique Calvo (bl). **Getty Images:** Handout (c); Gerard Malie / AFP (tl). **Rex by Shutterstock:** Dimitris Tossidis / Intime / Athena (bl). **88 Alamy Stock Photo:** irishphoto.com (cra); Keystone Pictures USA (cl). **89 Alamy Stock Photo:** Epa B.v. / Naeem Ul Haq (clb); epa european pressphoto agency b.v. (tl); Luciano Movio (cr). **92 Alamy Stock Photo:** GL Archive (cl). **Getty Images:** Bettmann (bl). **92-93 Alamy Stock Photo:** Hi-Story (c). **Dreamstime.com:** Hupeng (c/Motor-wagen). **93 Alamy Stock Photo:** Hi-Story (tl); Keystone Pictures USA (bc). **Courtesy Mercedes-Benz Cars, Daimler AG:** Mercedes-Benz Classic (tr). **94-95 Bridgeman Images:** Museum of the City of New York, USA (c). **94 Getty Images:** Fotosearch / Archive Photos (c). **Library of Congress, Washington, D.C.:** (cl). **95 Alamy Stock Photo:** Photo Researchers Inc (tl, clb, cra); Wenn Ltd (bc). **Getty Images:** Anthony Barboza / Archive Photos (bc). **96 Alamy Stock Photo:** Granger Historical Picture Archive (tr). **Getty Images:** Keystone-France / Gamma-Keystone (clb); Chicago Tribune / Tribune News Service (cr). **Photoshot:** R4610 / Picture Alliance (crb). **97 Alamy Stock Photo:** Dinodia Photos (tl); Xinhua (c). **98 Alamy Stock Photo:** Peter Horree (cr). **Dreamstime.com:** Leonid Andronov (bc). **Getty Images:** Francis G. Mayer (bl); George Rinhart (c). **99 123RF.com:** Eric Isselee (crb, crb/Lhasa); Erik Lam (crb/Lhasa Apso). **Alamy Stock Photo:** steven gillis hd9 imaging (cra). **Getty Images:** Ron Galella (tl); Venturelli (bc). **Photoshot:** Patrick McMullan / LFI (cr). **100-101 123RF.com:** skdesign (cb). **100 Getty Images:** Laurence Agron (tr). **Alamy Stock Photo:** Apic / Hulton Archive (bl). **Rex by Shutterstock:** (c). **101 Alamy Stock Photo:** Paul Velgos (tc). **Dreamstime.com:** Featureflash (bc); Jaguarps (cla). **Photoshot:** Everett (bl). **102 Alamy Stock Photo:** Richard Ellis (c). **Images Copyright 2012 by Katy Dickinson. All Rights Reserved:** (cb). **103 Alamy Stock Photo:** Britta Pedersen / dpa picture alliance (tc). **Getty Images:** Bloomberg (bc). **Photoshot:** David Wimsett (cra). **106-107 Getty Images:** Keystone / Hulton Archive (c). **106 Alamy Stock Photo:** Granger Historical Picture Archive (cl). **Library of Congress, Washington, D.C.:** (bc). **Press Association Images:** Tom Fitzsimmons / AP (bl). **107 Alamy Stock Photo:** Diane Johnson (tr). **Dreamstime.com:** Eagleflying (bc). **Getty Images:** Bettmann (cra). **108-109 Alamy Stock Photo:** Granger Historical Picture Archive (c). **108 Alamy Stock Photo:** Granger Historical Picture Archive (cl). **SuperStock:** Universal Images Group (bc). **Wellcome Images http://creativecommons.org/licenses/by/4.0/:** Archives & Manuscripts (bl). **Wikipedia:** Thurston, George H. (1876) Pittsburgh and Allegheny in the Centennial Year, Pittsburgh: A.A. Anderson & Son, bet. pp. 262 and 263 (tc). **109 Alamy Stock Photo:** Granger Historical Picture Archive (tc). **Dreamstime.com:** Ariwasabi (cr); Italianestro (c). **Getty Images:** Imagno / Hulton Archive (bl); Michel Porro (tr). **Library of Congress, Washington, D.C.:** (cb). **110 Dorling Kindersley:** The Shuttleworth Collection (c). **Getty Images:** Heritage Images / Hulton Archive (br). **Library of Congress, Washington, D.C.:** Bain Collection (bl). **111 Alamy Stock Photo:** Pictorial Press Ltd (cra); Sputnik (bl). **Dorling Kindersley:** Roy Palmer (cr). **ESA:** (clb). **Getty Images:** New York Times Co. (tc). **112 Dreamstime.com:** Italianestro (cr). **Mary Evans Picture Library:** (cl). **Photoshot:** UPPA (bc). **Wellcome Images http://creativecommons.org/licenses/by/4.0/:** Rare Books (tr). **112-113 Photoshot:** (c). **113 123RF.com:** Ievgenii Fesenko (crb). **Alamy Stock Photo:** GL Archive (clb); Keystone Pictures USA (bc). **Getty Images:** Ron Burton / Hulton Archive (bl); Danita Delimont (tr). **114 Alamy Stock Photo:** Granger Historical Picture Archive (bc). **Getty Images:** Science & Society Picture Library (bl). **115 Alamy Stock Photo:** Norbert Eisele-Hein / imageBROKER (bc). **Getty Images:** Europa Press (bl); Keystone / Hulton Archive (cla). **116 Alamy Stock Photo:** Bettmann (c, bl); Keystone / Hulton Archive (ca). **117 Dreamstime.com:** Ecophoto (cb). **Getty Images:** Darren England (c). **Press Association Images:** Alan Porritt / Aap (clb). **118 Getty Images:** ullstein bild (bc); Ken Levine (cla). **Photoshot:** World History Archive (bc). **119 Alamy Stock Photo:** PCN Photography (cl, bc). **Getty Images:** Bettmann (bl). **120 Getty Images:** AFP (cr). **Photoshot:** Gary Lee (cr). **121 Alamy Stock Photo:** Matthew Taylor (cra). **Getty Images:** Andy Lyons (crb); Ian Walton (cla, fcl, cl). **122 Getty Images:** Buda Mendes (cl); Popperfoto (bl, bc). **122-123 Getty Images:** Anadolu Agency (cl). **123 Alamy Stock Photo:** Tommy E Trenchard (cra). **Getty Images:** Evening Standard (tr). **Getty Images:** Evening Standard / Hulton Archive (bl)

All other images © Dorling Kindersley
For further information see: www.dkimages.com